DATE DUE

DEC 6 1999			
MAY 2 9 2003			

DEMCO 38-297

PATRICIA RAIN

VANILLA

COOKBOOK

Photographs by
BENJAMIN H. KAESTNER, III

CELESTIAL ARTS
BERKELEY CALIFORNIA

Celestial Arts
P.O. Box 7327
Berkeley, CA 94707

Interior photography by Benjamin H. Kaestner III, McCormick & Co., Inc.
Cover photography by Bill Schwob
Cover and interior design by Ken Scott
Typography by Ann Flanagan Typography
Production by Hugh Swift

Made in the United States of America

Library of Congress Cataloging in Publication Data

Rain, Patricia, 1943–
   Patricia Rain's Vanilla cookbook.
   Includes index.
   1. Cookery (Vanilla) 2. Vanilla. I. Title.
II. Title: Vanilla cookbook.
TX819.V35R35 1986   641.6'382   85-29149
ISBN 0-89087-453-0

First Printing, 1986

2 3 4 5 — 96 95 94 93

CONTENTS

ACKNOWLEDGEMENTS

A number of people were instrumental in helping to bring this book to fruition. I am most grateful for each person's contribution.

I want to thank Jerry Goodman for suggesting that I write this book, and for his assistance with information and recipes.

My gratitude and thanks to Bert Greene, Maida Heatter, Margaret Fox, Lisa Tanner, Philip Farar, Greg Reynolds, Mary-Pat Tormey, Verena La Mar, Eleanor Lewallen, and Karen Delee for permission to use their recipes in this book, and to M.F.K. Fisher for introducing me to Bert Greene's *Kitchen Bouquets* after trying to convince me that anything that is good with vanilla is even better with rum!

Special thanks to the research staff of the Half Moon Bay and Menlo Park libraries, and to the staff of the La Honda Post Office, for always helping out when I'm desperate or late. And special thanks also to Phil Wood, David Hinds, and my editor Paul Reed, and the rest of the staff at Celestial Arts/Ten Speed Press for their unconditional support.

Last, but most importantly, thanks and love to my mother, Katie, for giving me an empty bottle of vanilla extract when I was five along with permission to cook in the kitchen on my own (and with a full bottle of extract) when I wasn't much older; to my father Buzz, and my brother John, for the praise they gave me when I cooked for them, and for eating the disasters as well as the successes without complaining, and to my husband Robert, and my daughter Serena, who acted as food testers and critics as we ate our way through the following recipes. It is to my family that I dedicate this book.

TAHITIAN IMPORT / EXPORT, INC. is pleased to bring you a copy of *The Vanilla Cookbook*.

Since 1982 TAHITIAN IMPORT / EXPORT, INC. has been dedicated to importing, distributing, and manufacturing the finest quality beans and extracts. Our beans come from Tahiti and other South Pacific Islands, and our extracts are made entirely from premium quality beans. If one classifies synthetic vanilla as being one dimensional and most commercial extracts as being two dimensional, then our premium natural vanilla would have to be multi-dimensional.

Our goal is to educate both amateur and professional chefs about the benefits of using superior-quality natural ingredients. By doing a taste comparison, we are certain that you will experience the difference between TAHITIAN IMPORT / EXPORT, INC. vanilla and other extracts and beans.

We welcome any questions or comments you may have.

Bon Appetite   Tamaa Maitai

INTRODUCTION

When I was five years old, I set up a small outdoor dwelling on the terraced garden below our house. The only room was a "kitchen" where I "cooked" flowers and candies and whatever else I could appropriate from the main house. One of my treasured possessions was a small empty brown bottle that had contained pure vanilla extract.

I loved that little bottle and its fragrant memory. It fit well in my small hand; it had a little cap that twisted on and off; and, most importantly, when it was opened, I was enchanted by its rich perfume. The scent never conjured up exotic images—everything was perfect as is while I sat on the warm earth, surrounded by lantana, hollyhocks, and roses. Vanilla was the "magic" in the small brown bottle. I needed no further explanation.

When my friend Jerry Goodman suggested that I consider writing a book on vanilla, however, I was skeptical. I wasn't certain there would be enough of a story to warrant a whole book devoted to such an everyday item as vanilla. What I discovered, however, as I began the research that ultimately led to this book, was that the small brown bottle that had intrigued and delighted me was far more exotic and magical than I could have ever imagined.

To give you a taste, so to speak, of its exotic and magical qualities, consider the following:

Vanilla comes from the fruit of an orchid which is native to tropical America. It is the most labor-intensive agricultural product in the world—from planting the vine to bottling the aged extract is a five year process, and each step of the process up to extraction must be done by hand.

Even in its native habitat, vanilla was a rare and precious commodity. The Aztecs, who subjugated and taxed the Totonacs—the Indians responsible for discovering and processing vanilla—considered it a gift from the gods and could afford it only for the rituals of the Aztec nobility.

In Madagascar, now the largest vanilla growing area in the world, vanilla beans are still so valuable that *each* bean is branded with the owner's special mark to protect it from "vanilla rustlers."

The molecular structure of the vanilla bean is so complex that to this day not all of the compounds that contribute to the unique flavor and aroma of vanilla have been isolated and identified. This is why there is no synthetic that comes close to exacting the true flavor of pure vanilla. The unique scent and flavor that we recognize as vanilla does not, however, exist in the bean at the time of harvest. It must be processed and cured to develop this scent and flavor.

Vanilla was at one time considered *the* quintessential flavor; it was equated with the extraordinary. As our lives have become so filled with sensory delights of all kinds, our culture has essentially demoted vanilla. It is now equated by many as bland, ordinary, or generic.

But consider this. When vanilla and chocolate were first introduced to Europe in the 16th century, sugar was a rare delicacy, coffee and tea were available only to the wealthy and titled, and cloves, cinnamon, nutmeg, and pepper were expensive commodities. Vanilla and chocolate were only available to royalty, and even then, only in limited quantities.

When vanilla and chocolate finally became available to the masses, chocolate could only be purchased as cocoa powder, and vanilla only as a bean. It wasn't until the second half of the 19th century that bar chocolate and vanilla extract were developed. In other words, pure vanilla extract has been a commonplace household flavor in the United States for only about 100 years!

Although I still cherish sitting in the sun on the warm earth in my garden, the majority of my cooking is done indoors, and my bottles of pure vanilla extract and jars of beans are well provisioned. The magic I now get from vanilla is knowing how to use the beans and pure extract in a manner that approximates culinary alchemy. For instance, not only does vanilla enhance the sweetness of a food, it also mellows the flavor of eggs, cuts the acidity of lemon and pineapple, and accentuates and "lifts" chocolate. It enlivens both sweet *and* savory foods, can be used with equal success in raw, cooked, or baked dishes, and provides its own subtle flavor that mingles delicately with other ingredients.

It was an enlightening and gratifying experience to discover that vanilla indeed warranted a full book devoted to its exotic story and unique qualities. It is my hope that you will be as amazed and delighted as I was as you read the stories and sample the recipes contained on these pages. And I would venture to say that when you have completed this book, you will likely agree that vanilla is still *the* quintessential flavor, or, as the Totonacs have believed for centuries, vanilla is truly the nectar of the gods.

Patricia Rain

HISTORY OF VANILLA

It is not known with any certainty just how the vanilla bean was discovered as a flavor or how the techniques for processing vanilla were developed. But several tribes living in southeastern Mexico may have discovered vanilla at least 1,000 years ago, possibly much before that.

It is possible that monkeys were observed chewing vanilla beans that had ripened fully and fallen to the jungle floor and fermented. Perhaps some adventurous individual picked up a fermented bean, and, smelling the natural vanillin triggered by the fermentation, tried the bean, liked it, and began to incorporate it into the tribal diet.

However the discovery was made, by the time the Aztecs conquered the indigenous tribes of this area, the local Indians had developed a system for processing the beans using a crude fermentation technique.

The Aztecs were quite enchanted by the vanilla flavor, and so they required that the Totonac and other local tribes grow the beans for them. The beans were then used as a method of paying tribute to the Emperor. Even at this early date vanilla beans were a rare and precious commodity, much the same as cocoa beans, and were used as money. Vanilla beans were also used as a source of perfume and as an herbal medicinal tonic.

Hernan Cortez was the first white man to taste vanilla, in Mexico, in 1520.

When Colombus returned to Spain and told of his accidental discoveries, the Spanish government wanted a cut of the action. Within 10 years a Spanish colony was firmly established in Cuba, and an appeal was made to young men interested in exploring and settling these new lands. Exploratory trips were made and goods brought back by ship. In 1510, vanilla beans were brought to Europe along with indigo and cochineal dyes and cocoa beans. Apparently vanilla was not identified as a flavoring, but rather as a perfume, and there is no evidence that it was known to be used for anything else.

In 1520, Cortes—one of the young Spaniards who wished to explore and conquer the New World—landed with his army on the southeast coast of Mexico. They quickly defeated the local people, and then, with the help of 10,000 Tlascalan Indians, arch rivals of the Aztecs, they began trekking toward Tenochtitlan, the Aztec Capital of Mexico.

After several months they arrived in Tenochtitlan, fully expecting an army to greet them with warfare. Instead, the civilized Montezuma greeted them with graciousness befitting royalty. The Spaniards resembled the long-time Aztec prophecy about fair-skinned, blond-haired gods who would arrive from the East. Cortes knew nothing of the prophecy, and was impressed by Montezuma's welcome.

Bernal Diaz, an observant and educated soldier travelling with Cortes was quick to note that Montezuma drank *chocolatl,* a beverage made from powdered cocoa beans and ground corn, flavored with *tlilxochitl* (the Aztec word for black vanilla pods), and honey. Hernan Cortes was himself served this royal beverage, according to legend, in golden goblets with golden spoons (the mixture was supposedly quite thick and would slowly dissolve in the mouth. Although Diaz was filled in on the ingredients by the court, the Aztecs were not especially keen on releasing the secrets on how the drink was flavored and prepared.

Despite the warm welcome, Cortes had arrived to conquer the Aztecs, and ultimately Montezuma lost his life, city, and his beloved beverage, along with the gold and silver.

It is somewhat unclear whether or not Cortes and his entourage were aware that vanilla was an essential part of the flavoring of *chocolatl.* Some accounts say that Cortes took vanilla back to Spain and presented it to the king. Other accounts credit Bernardino de Sahagun, a Franciscan friar who went to Mexico in 1529, for instructing the Europeans about *tlilxochitl.* Sahagun did write a *General History of the Things of New Spain,* which he originally wrote in the Aztec language, which was supposedly available in Europe in 1560. Curiously, the work was not published in Mexico until 300 years after it was written.

However the Europeans discovered that vanilla was a flavoring agent, factories were established for manufacturing chocolate with vanilla as early as the second half of the 16th century.

In 1571, King Phillip II sent Francisco Hernandez on a mission to Mexico. During the six years Hernandez spent in Mexico, he became an authority on vanilla. In his work *Rerum Medicarum Novae Hispaniae Thesaurus,* published in Rome in 1651, he identified the plant as "*Araco aromatico.*" He noted that the beans were used by the Mexicans not only for their pleasant taste and aroma, but also for their alleged healing qualities.

In the meantime, Carolus Clusius wrote about the vanilla pods in 1605 after receiving some untreated beans from Hugh Morgan, apothecary to Queen Elizabeth I. He named the beans *Lobus oblongus aromaticus.* He commented that they smelled like benzoin, strongly enough to provoke headaches (they had probably begun to ferment and decompose).

It wasn't until 1658 that William Piso wrote that the Spaniards used the beans, which they called "vaynilla," meaning "little pod." This was supposedly the first time that the word "vaynilla," from which the scientific name of the genus comes, was used.

It was during the latter part of the 16th century that vanilla became quite popular among the royalty and the monied of Europe. Vanilla was always considered an adjunct to chocolate, however, until 1602, when Hugh Morgan suggested that vanilla be used as a flavoring by itself. Queen Elizabeth was extraordinarily fond of vanilla, so much so that as an old woman she would eat and drink only foods prepared with vanilla.

The Spanish used vanilla as a flavoring for chocolate for a short time, but then abandoned it in favor of cinnamon. Not so the French. They adored vanilla, and by the 18th century vanilla was used in France more than any other European country—both as a flavoring for chocolate, for confections and ices, as well as for scenting perfumes and tobacco.

According to Waverly Root, in *Food* (Simon and Schuster 1980), Thomas Jefferson discovered vanilla during his stay in France. When he returned to the United States in 1789 to establish himself as Secretary of State in Philadelphia (which was at that time the national capital) he missed vanilla very much. When he sent his French aide to the market to get him some vanilla beans, the aide returned saying that no one in Philadelphia knew what they were. Jefferson then wrote to William Short, the American *charge d'affaires* in Paris, to send him 50 pods wrapped in the middle of a packet of newspapers. Short must have sent him the pods, because for quite a long time Philadelphia had the reputation for the finest vanilla ice cream in the world.

It was during the 18th century that cuttings of the vanilla plants were taken or smuggled (depending upon whose point of view was being expressed) out of Mexico and Central America, with hopes of being able to grow the vine either in Europe or in the tropical colonial outposts of the various countries. Cuttings were started with success around 1730, but the plants seldom flowered and never produced fruits. It was rumored that there was a curse placed on the plants by Montezuma, and that they would never fruit in areas other than their native habitat.

Then, suddenly in 1807, a vine in the collection of the Right Honorable Charles Greville, at Paddington, England, not only produced flowers, but fruited as well. This is the first record of a vanilla fruit having been produced in Europe, and in retrospect, no one knows quite how it occurred.

The famous illustrator, Frank Bauer, drew the plant with its fruit, and the botanical gardens of Paris and Antwerp were supplied with cuttings from this spectacular plant. It caused great fervor, especially because the phenomenon did not recur the following year.

Attempts to grow the *cuttings* in Java and other tropical areas proved successful, but again, no fruit appeared. Then, finally in 1836, Charles Morren, a botanist from Belgium, solved the mystery. He observed the plants in their native habitat and discovered that the flowers needed to be individually pollinated in order to fruit. This was done naturally by a very small bee, the melipona, and by species of hummingbirds. It may also have been done by ants. As these native Mexican insects and birds were not taken with the plant cuttings, no pollination occurred. Additionally, it was later discovered that the Totonac Indians had been aware of this all along.

With this discovery, the opportunity to grow vanilla in other tropical areas was finally a reality. In 1841, a former slave from the French island of Reunion, Edmond Albius, perfected a method of hand pollination. With the pointed tip of a small bamboo stick, he transferred the male pollen masses to the sticky female stigma inside the flower. This same method of artificial pollination is still used today.

Plantations for growing vanilla were quickly developed in Madagascar, Reunion (formerly the Bourbon Islands), Mauritius, the Seychelles Islands, Tahiti, the Comoro Islands, Ceylon, Java, the Philippines, and parts of Africa, as well as throughout the West Indies. Attempts were made to grow vanilla in India and China, and although it grew there, it never became a commercial enterprise. By the 19th century, more vanilla was being produced in tropical Asia and Madagascar than in Mexico, thus breaking the monopoly which had been held by Mexico, Central America, and the West Indies for over 200 years.

Today Madagascar, the Comoro Islands, and Reunion, producing the top quality "Bourbon" vanilla, grow 80 percent of the world's crop of vanilla beans. The remainder is grown largely in Bali, Tonga, Tahiti, and Mexico. Ironically, Mexico, once the head of vanilla production, can now barely produce enough vanilla for its own internal use. Lands that were once ideal cultivation areas have been over-harvested and converted to oil fields, citrus groves, and cattle grazing land. Ancestors of the Totonac Indians still work on the vanilla plantations, but it is difficult to grow the vines in the vastly altered countryside.

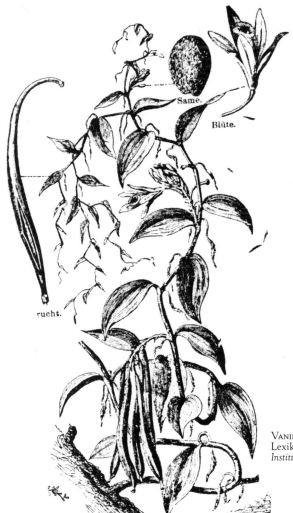

VANILLA. *Engraving from Meyers:*
Lexikon, *Bibliographisches*
Institut, Leipzig, 1897

BOTANICAL INFORMATION

Vanilla comes from the fruit of a
thick tropical vine which is a member
of the orchid family, *Orchidacae,* the
largest family of flowering plants in
the world. Of the 35,000 or more
species in this family, the vanilla orchid
produces the only edible fruit. It is
often called the orchid of commerce
because it is one of the two products
of this enormous species with any sig-
nificant commercial value. (Commercially grown orchids are the other
product.)

Interestingly, not only is the vanilla
orchid devoid of scent, so is the vanilla pod or bean, which must be fermented or cured to develop the
vanillin—the primary flavor of vanilla
—encased within. Vanilla vines thrive
in any area about 25 degrees north
or south of the Equator, or as far north
as eastern Mexico and south as Madagascar. Vanilla does best in warm,
moist climates, with a mixture of
shade and sunshine, and grows well
from sea level to about 2000 feet. In

Mexico, vines have been found growing at 3,500 feet but the best quality plants are found at lower altitudes. The ideal conditions for vanilla vines are moderate rainfall, evenly distributed over ten months of the year, with a two month dry season to encourage flower-budding and fruiting; gently sloping land to insure water runoff; about 50% each sunlight and shade; and no extended periods of drought. Drought will cause the orchids to drop before forming correctly and will hinder or stop the growth of the beans.

Vanilla vines are indigenous to southeastern Mexico, the West Indies, Central America, and northern South America. There are over 50 species of vanilla orchid, but only three have been used commercially: *Vanilla planifolia*, *Vanilla pompona*, and *Vanilla tahitensis*.

Vanilla planifolia, formerly known as *Vanilla fragrans*, is by far the most important of the species, and produces almost all of the vanilla used in the United States. The less important *Vanilla pompona*, is more resistant to root rot disease and flowers one to two years after planting whereas *Vanilla planifolia* flowers three to four years after planting, but the *Vanilla pompona* beans are inferior in quality. *Vanilla tahitensis* is cultivated from the French Oceania group of islands in the Pacific. It is suspected that Tahiti vanilla was originally brought to French Polynesia from Mexico several hundred years ago. Since all other vanilla species are found in Latin America, this suspicion is probably well-founded. Tahiti vanilla pods are shorter and have a thicker skin and lower seed count than those of *Vanilla planifolia*, and are quite broad in the middle, tapering to both ends. *Vanilla tahitensis* is primarily exported to France and to Europe.

The vines of the vanilla plant climb to the tops of tall trees in the jungle, often 50 to 80 feet in height. The plant has a simple or branched, succulent stem with aerial roots opposite the leaves, which cling to the tree or other supports to hold the vines up. The leaves of the perennial vine are bright green in color, flat, wide, and smooth. Clusters of 20 or more buds are produced on the short stalks in the angle between leaf and stem. It may take as long as six weeks for the bud to develop into a flower. The satiny greenish-yellow orchid will flower in the morning and begin to wilt by early afternoon. If the orchid is not pollinated, it will usually drop from the plant by early evening. A healthy vanilla vine may produce as many as a thousand blossoms, but only the ones that are pollinated—from 50 to 300, depending upon the age and health of the plant—will develop into pods or beans.

The beans are long and slender and cylindrical in shape, and filled with thousands of tiny, edible seeds. The beans, green at first, become yellow on the tips and reach a length of 4 to 12 inches by the time they are ready to be picked at about 8 or 9 months. If allowed to fully ripen, the beans will turn golden yellow and will split open.

Most writers explain that the generic name *vanilla* is derived from the Spanish *vainilla*, meaning sheath, little scabbard, or pod. The immediate etymology is from *vaina*, or string bean. Upon further investigation, however, the original word source come from the Latin, *vagina*. Curiously, the root word of orchid, *orchis*, is Greek, and means testicle. Further, the Aztecs considered the vanilla bean to be a powerful aphrodisiac as did the Europeans. As you have likely ascertained by now, that benign looking brown bottle of liquid on the pantry shelf has a rather sexy background!

The *vanillin* produced in the vanilla bean is also found naturally in a few other plants. The ponderosa pine and some other coniferous trees contain vanillin in the bark, and vanillin can also be found in the sapwood of firs, and from lignin, removed from wood pulp in the process of paper making. Vanillin is only one of the more than 150 organic chemical components that make up the fragrance and flavor of vanilla, and therefore the vanillin from the conifer and its by-products can only partially emulate the taste of true vanilla.

Another vanilla-like substance comes from coumarin. Deer's Tongue, also known as *Wild Vanilla* and *Vanilla Leaf,* is a perennial plant native to North America. It has a strong vanilla odor which is largely attributed to coumarin which forms crystals on the upper side of the leaves. *Deer's Tongue* was used to scent tobacco, and as a medicinal. Sweet clover and woodruff also contain coumarin and have a somewhat vanilla-like odor.

Probably the largest source of natural coumarin comes from the tonka bean, the fruit of a forest tree native to Brazil and British Guiana *(Dipteryx odorata),* and known in Latin America as *Rumara.* Coumarin is often used as a substitute for vanilla in perfumery, to disguise the taste of medicines, and also as a substitute for vanilla extract. In Holland the fatty substance of the beans has been sold as Tonquin butter.

Coumarin has a medicinal component, *dicumarol,* an anticoagulant used in blood-thinning medicines. *Dicumarol* is closely related to the chemical *warfarin,* used in rat poisons as it causes internal hemorrhaging. It is also narcotic and can cause liver and kidney damage or paralyze the heart if used in large doses. The FDA banned coumarin's use in food in the United States in 1954. It is used in Mexico, however, as a major ingredient in the inexpensive "vanillas" sold throughout the country. Added to natural vanilla or vanillin, coumarin enhances the flavor which, along with the low cost, makes it appealing to unsuspecting tourists seeking the famed Mexican vanilla. For information about choosing quality vanilla extracts as well as determining synthetics, see my chapter on "How to Purchase, Store, and Use Vanilla Extracts and Beans," page 15.

CULTIVATION, HARVESTING, CURING, AND GRADING

There are three major vanilla producing areas from which the United States gets most of its vanilla. The islands in the Indian Ocean—Madagascar, the Comoro Islands and Reunion—produce the "Bourbon" bean, which was the original name for Reunion (which was named for the Bourbon Kings of Europe). It is from these islands that roughly 3,000,000 pounds of the world's vanilla beans are produced. The United States is importing an average of 1,500,000 pounds of cured vanilla beans yearly from these islands, which accounts for 80% to 85% of annual U.S. purchases.

Most of the Madagascar vanilla is grown by the Malagasy on vanilla plantations. Nearly all vanilla production occurs on the northeast coast of the island, centered around the town of Antalaha. The vanilla growing area is barely 100 miles north to south, and it extends inland about 25 miles from the coast. The plants

flower from October to December and are harvested between July and September.

The freshly picked beans are bought by middlemen who classify the beans and cure them. After curing, the vanilla crop is handled by the Madagascar government, which acts as exporter.

In 1964, the government of Madagascar decided that year-to-year fluctuations in the supply and price of beans were causing user nations, such as the United States, to resort, in part, to the use of synthetics. A price stabilization board was established, and a vanilla "bank" was created. The "bank" regulates the flow of beans, assuring a constant supply, setting the price, transacting the sales, and passing specified percentages of the proceeds back to the growers, curers, brokers and "packer-storers" (as the final members of the chain are called).

Taxes are collected from sales of the beans. This tax maintains the "bank." Each packer-storer houses quantities of government registered stock which are put away during times of surplus to be released when supplies are low.

The second largest area of production is in Indonesia, producing a fluctuating supply of 8% to 25% of U.S. vanilla imports, or roughly 300,000 pounds per year. The beans are mainly produced on Bali, but are known as "Java" beans.

Originally "Java" vanilla was grown in Central and Eastern Java, but there was a severe problem with theft which forced the growers to harvest the beans long before they were ready. Consequently the vanillin content of the beans was quite low. In recent years, the vanilla growing area has been moved to the island of Bali.

The local Hindu religion, plus the somewhat less populated land area, have resulted in less robbery, and the beans are sometimes able to stay on the vines until they have more fully matured.

In general, Java vanilla is of inferior quality and is only used legitimately for blends of real and imitation vanilla used in vanilla "flavored" ice cream. Some unscrupulous vanilla extractors, however, have taken Java beans, added adulturants, and then sold it as pure vanilla extract.

Although Mexico no longer produces an abundance of vanilla—indeed, it can't produce enough even for its own internal use—it is the original source of the crop, and its techniques for producing vanilla have been copied all over the world with few adaptations. Mexican beans are also considered by many to be the best in the world. For this reason, Mexican vanilla beans are considered among the top three worldwide. But Mexico produces only about 10 tons of beans annually, and the United States gets less than 1% of its annual pruchases from Mexico.

Mexican vanilla is grown in the state of Vera Cruz. The town of Gutierrez Zamora, located on the northern bank of the Tecolutla River, is a major curing center, and there are several plants there for making extracts (currently only one is making pure vanilla extract).

The Totonac Indians, descendants of the first growers, have an almost intuitive sense about the vanilla vines and the growing process. The jungle canopy which once shaded the vines and provided moisture and protection is now largely gone, and therefore growing conditions are more difficult.

Roads were built into this area in the 1940's. Before that, beans were transported, mainly by river, to the coast, where they travelled by schooner to Vera Cruz or Tampico. The other route was by mule pack over mountain trails to the railhead at Tezuitlan, and then by train to Vera Cruz or Laredo. Since the advent of highways, bananas have replaced some of the crops in the lowland areas, but vanilla is still grown as well.

The Totonacs were apparently among the first to pledge allegiance to Cortes and consequently were left undisturbed in the private ownership of their individual tracts. Their lands were primarily on the first rising ground on the coastal plain of the Gulf of Mexico. The Totonacs were also known as good bargainers, and traditionally they demanded payment in silver, which they then buried in the ground. They also controlled the production of the beans, increasing or reducing the crops with the rise and fall in prices.

This has all changed. They are now the *workers* on the vanilla plantations, with only a small section of land for a home and garden. They grow a few vines of their own for pocket money, but other than that, they have no control over the vanilla crops.

In Mexico, the plants flower in April and May, and the beans are harvested from the end of November to January. There is a large festival at the end of the harvest.

There are a few other vanilla producing areas. Tahiti produces 5 to 10 tons of beans a year, but the majority of this crop goes to Europe. Tonga is beginning to establish itself as a vanilla producing island, and the quality of the beans can be as good as the beans from Madagascar if properly cured, but the United States still gets less than 1% of U.S. imports from Tonga.

Vanilla growing, curing, and processing is the most labor intensive of all agricultural products. It even exceeds saffron (the most expensive spice in the world). Like most agricultural products, vanilla is also subject to loss due to adverse weather conditions and disease. Regardless, for most of the growers it's the best, or only, game in town.

Vanilla grows best in the tropical areas up to 25 degrees on either side of the equator. A warm, moist climate with regular rainfall is necessary.

The land used for growing vanilla should be humus rich and with good drainage. A gently rising slope is ideal. Small trees are used for the vanilla vines to climb and to provide shade for the vines. The selection of the trees used depends largely on local conditions, but the general rule of thumb is for small-leaved trees which allow filtered light through to the vines. Trees that grow rapidly are preferable, and ones that have low branches (between 5 and 7 feet from the ground) are ideal, so that the vines are within easy reach of the workers. The trees should be strong enough to withstand strong winds (cyclones are a serious problem in Madagascar), and should never lose all their leaves at one time. The trees are planted about a year or more before the vanilla cuttings are set so that they can become well established. Fast growing banana plants and corn are sometimes grown alongside the vines in Mexico to provide shade for the young vines. An evergreen called *filao* is the preferred tree in Madagascar.

Since the seeds do not germinate easily in nature, vanilla is grown from cuttings. Cuttings of one meter are standard. The plants will not bear flowers or fruit until the third or fourth year.

In the early days of vanilla growing, plants were grown very close together and the plants intertwined. Enormous crops were produced until disease struck the plants, and many plantations were totally wiped out as there was no way to separate the diseased plants from the healthy. It is now standard practice to place the supporting trees about 5 to 9 feet apart, and to have 1 or 2 vines per tree. This allows for between 530 and 870 vines per acre. The vines are checked at least once every 2 weeks when they are first growing in order to prune and train them. They are looped over the tree at the 5 foot level and brought back down to the ground to keep them at a level the workers can easily reach. As long as the vine can grow upward it won't flower, so the tip of the vine is cut off 9 or 10 months before the flowering season.

The vines reach their maximum production about the 7th or 8th year, but if properly cared for, will produce for several more years.

Once the plants flower, they receive daily attention. The flowers are hand pollinated, and excess buds, blossoms, and extra pods are removed so that the plant will have the vitality to produce the best quality pods.

The plants are usually pollinated by women and children, as they are quick with their hands and able to reach into the flowers easily. In Madagascar, the hand pollinating process is called "the marriage of vanilla." An average worker may hand pollinate from 1,000 to 2,000 flowers a day. Although each plant could produce up to 1,000 beans per crop, the actual number of flowers that are pollinated varies from about 50 to 300, depending on the age and health of the plant. This helps to ensure an even crop each year, because the plant will become "exhausted" if forced to produce too much in any given year.

The bean will get the bulk of its full length in 4 to 8 weeks, but it takes 8 to 9 months for the beans to mature completely. Because of the demand for the beans, and also because of the problem of theft, many growers in some areas try to harvest their crops early. The governments of most areas have regulations to prevent early harvesting, but these are difficult to enforce. In Madagascar, where theft had been a consistent problem, the beans are often branded with the growers specifc mark. This is done with pins stuck into a cork or with a signet ring. The pin pricks remain on the beans, even after curing, appearing as tiny yellowish-tan scars on the dark brown surface.

The beans are firm, thick, yellowish-green, and odorless when they are ready to be harvested. The tips are golden. The following account, written in 1912, describes what happens if the fruit is allowed to remain on the vine:

If left on the plant, the pod begins to turn yellow at the lower end and gives off an odour of bitter almonds. The pod begins to split into two unequal halves, and a small quantity of dark balsamic oil of a brown or red colour is produced. Gradually the pod darkens in colour from brown to black. The epidermis softens and the real vanilla odour develops. The oil, which is called "balsam of vanilla," then increases in quantity. This balsam is carefully collected by the planters in Peru and other parts of South America, but not sent to Europe. The pods, ripening slowly, upwards from the tip, take about a month to fully ripen. Eventually, if left, the pods become dry and black and brittle, and are then scentless.

During the harvest season the plants are checked daily. Some pickers use a sharp knife to gather the beans, while others use the thumb and middle finger to make a clean cut from the vine.

There are several techniques used to cure the beans. In Mexico and the Madagascar area, the sun is used, which is the ideal way to finish the ripening process. In Java, however, beans are smoked. The purpose of curing is to obtain uniformly cured and unsplit beans as rapidly as possible. Using a process of sweating and drying the pods, the beans will lose up to 80% of their moisture.

The curing should begin within a week after the harvest. In some places the grower will cure his own beans, but usually the beans are taken to a facility where they are professionally cured.

In Mexico, the fruits are stored in sheds for a few days until they begin to shrivel. If the weather is good, the beans are spread on woolen blankets and placed in the sun for a few hours. When the beans are too hot to hold, the blanket is folded over them for the rest of the day. At the end of the day the bundles of beans are taken to blanket-lined, air-tight containers where they sweat all night. This process, which may take more than 2 weeks, is repeated until the beans turn a dark brown.

If the weather is cloudy or rainy, the beans are wrapped in blankets, sprinkled with water, and warmed in an oven. They are also alternately sweated and placed in the oven until they have turned brown.

After sweating, the beans are spread out on grass mats in the sun every day for 2 months or more, and then they are spread in a shelter until sufficiently dry and ready for market. In

Mexico, producing the perfect beans takes from 5 to 6 months.

In Madagascar, Comoro Islands, and Reunion, the curing process is the same with one exception. The curing process is begun by placing the beans in large baskets and dipping them for about 20 seconds in 190 degree water. This process stops the enzymatic process of ripening. The second step of alternately wrapping the beans and sun-drying them is done in the same way as in Mexico. The processing time is about 5 months.

In Indonesia, the beans are dried over wood fires, a process which only takes a few weeks. The problem with this technique is that the beans become stiff and lack the oily sheen of good beans. They also develop a smoky smell and taste.

There is a technique called "Potier's Process" which sounds fascinating, but is too expensive to be commercially feasible. The beans are soaked in rum for 20 to 30 days, then aired for 24 to 36 hours, during which time they never become totally dry. They are then shipped in the rum in which they were first soaked.

Beans that have been properly cured using the traditional methods should be supple enough to be twisted around the finger without tearing. To help in their suppleness, the beans are massaged to bring out some of the oils that form during fermentation. This is mainly done to the beans that remain whole and not to the beans destined to be used in extracts.

Vanilla beans are vulnerable to mold, especially if they have not been sufficiently dried. If they are dried and stored properly, however, they will last indefinitely.

After curing, the beans are sorted into several classes, mainly for quality, length, and moisture content, and then they are bundled by class, with 80 to 100 beans per bundle. Top grade beans are oily, smooth, aromatic, and a very dark brown. Occasionally there will be crystals of vanillin on the beans. Called *givre,* some people consider this a sign of excellence. (*Givre* is a french word that means "frost." The crystallization of the vanillin on the outside of the bean *looks* like the frost covering a lawn after a freeze. To some, it looks like mold, and novices can be fooled!)

After sorting, the beans are either sold in bulk or tied in bundles and packed in large tin boxes lined with waxed paper. In Bali, the beans are packed in cardboard with a plastic liner placed around that, and then with another cardboard box for shipping. The beans are now ready for shipment to the United States, Europe, and other markets.

THE EXTRACTION PROCESS

Vanilla *extract* is made by dissolving the essential flavor components of the beans in an alcohol-water mixture, and then separating the residue from the liquid.

The beans are first chopped in a machine that has knives suspended in the air to prevent any heat caused by friction. The mascerated beans are then placed in baskets and lowered into glass or stainless steel tanks. Using pumps, or a propellor at the bottom of the tank, the alcohol-water mixture (known as a *menstrum*) is continuously recirculated through the beans until the flavor is extracted, a process which takes 48 hours. Essentially, this process is the same as a percolator for coffee except that extreme heat is not used.

By heating the menstrum to about 130 degrees, the extract process can be completed more rapidly. Some manufacturers, however, feel that heat damages or destroys some of the delicate flavor of the vanilla, and so they prefer to process the menstrum at no higher than 60 degrees farenheit.

The menstrum is next "washed" twice to remove residue and alcohol and then is filtered into a holding tank where it will remain until it is bottled. Sugar is added to mellow the alcohol and to assist the aging of the extract. As little as 5% or as much as 40% of the extract will be sugar. Because extracts may vary somewhat in flavor and strength, they are tested and standardized. The finished extract is then aged before bottling.

The United States Food and Drug Administration (FDA) has established standards for the vanilla industry. In order to be labeled "*Pure Vanilla Extract*," the vanilla has to contain at least 35% alcohol by volume. Anything less is considered a "*flavor.*"

A standard vanilla extract must contain 13.35 ounces of vanilla beans to a gallon of 35% alcohol. A "2 fold" of pure vanilla contains 26.7 ounces of beans, a 3 fold," 40.05 ounces, and a "4 fold," 53.4 ounces of beans. To be called a vanilla *extract,* it must contain 35% minimum of alcohol. The industry's "20 fold" vanilla is called "20 fold vanilla concentrate" and contains no alcohol.

Pure vanilla flavors and pure vanilla extract have the same flavor; the difference is in the concentration of strength. The more highly concentrated extracts (sometimes 10 fold) are used for commercial baking and candymaking as some flavor is lost at high temperatures. Loss of flavor during cooking or baking is unlikely in regular home baking, as the ovens tend not to be quite so hot and less surface area is heated and used.

ABOUT TAHITIAN VANILLA

In the mid 1980s, while doing research for the first edition of this book, I received enthusiastic support from people involved in various aspects of the vanilla industry. However, whenever I asked any of these people about Tahitian vanilla, the responses invariably were an unenthusiastic, "It's a small crop and it all goes to France," or "It's an inferior bean, low in natural vanillin." Consequently, when press time came, I included only what little I had been told about Tahitian vanilla. I also made the supposition that as vanilla vines were planted by the French during their colonization of Tahiti, when hand pollinization was discovered, these same vines produced Vanilla tahitensis.

About four months after the book came out, I attended a food show in San Francisco where I met Peter Stone. Peter and his partner, Marc Jones, started Tahitian Import/Export Inc. in the early 1980s and were importing Tahitian vanilla for use in the United States. We spent several hours together talking (amazingly enough) about vanilla—primarily Tahitian vanilla. I was disappointed that I hadn't met him earlier, as I finally had the necessary information to properly complete this book. Finally, as I update this new edition, I can offer some solid, documented information about Tahitian vanilla.

The island of Tahiti produces only about ten to twelve tons of beans a year. However, when you realize that about five pounds of green beans yields one pound of finished beans, or about 120 pounds of finished beans per acre of vanilla vines, ten to twelve tons of finished beans are not insignificant as a cottage industry for a place as small as Tahiti.

Vanilla tahitensis pods are visually quite different from Vanilla planifolia. The beans tend to be shorter, have a thicker skin, fewer seeds and are much broader than the planifolia variety. They are reasonably low in natural vanillin but very high in floral components, especially the piperonals—a sweet, licorice-like flavor, also known as heliotropin.

The actual origins of Tahitian vanilla are uncertain. It may be that some Vanilla planifolia plant stock was hybridized or that it mutated, allegedly in a plant laboratory in the Philippines. Whichever occurred, it happened in the 1930s or early 1940s. Regardless or what transpired, Vanilla tahitensis is not indigenous to the South Pacific islands.

In the 1940s Tahitian farmers started growing vanilla as a cottage industry, mainly in small plots in their backyards. The farmers depended (and still do) on middlemen (usually Chinese) to cure the beans and sell them to the importers.

Because many importers felt that Tahitian vanilla was too low in natural vanillin content and too different in flavor to be used in extracts for the American consumer, until the 1980s France was the primary importer of Tahitian vanilla. Now, however, largely due to the educational efforts on the part of Peter and Marc, chefs, bakers, and home users of vanilla in the United States are increasingly using Tahitian vanilla for its distinctive floral flavor.

I personally don't consider Tahitian beans better or worse than Bourbon beans, just different. In fact, Tahitian vanilla is my first choice in anything containing fruit as well as in seafood, poultry, and wild game. I'm also more likely to use Tahitian vanilla if I'm adding a few drops of extract to fresh vegetables. I usually use Bourbon vanilla or a blend of Tahitian and Bourbon in pastries and other baked goods.

My suggestion to people wondering whether to purchase Bourbon or Tahitian vanilla is to get a small container of each and experiment. If that isn't possible, I suggest that if the traditional "vanilla" flavor is desired, use Bourbon vanilla. If you are open to new tastes or are fond of floral, fruity flavors, then buy Tahitian vanilla.

HOW TO PURCHASE, STORE AND USE VANILLA EXTRACTS AND BEANS

Pure vanilla extracts are available in supermarkets, specialty food stores, and through distributors. As there is some variance in quality, here are a few pointers for determining what you are purchasing. Also, the information in the glossary (page 19) provides an explanation of names and contents of the various grades of natural and synthetic products.

First, to make certain that you are getting pure vanilla extract, check the label. It *must* be labelled *"Pure Vanilla Extract"* and contain at least 35% alcohol. Vanilla extracts that contain sugar, coloring, or preservatives must also declare this on the label. It is not requried to list the percentage of sugar, however. As sugar speeds up the aging and mellowing process of the extract, some manufacturers will use 20% to 40% sugar in the extract. Also, some pure vanilla

extracts contain carmelized sugar. This gives the extract a dark or muddy appearance.

The finest quality extracts will have a rich perfumed smell, an amber color, and a low sugar content. Buy a small amount of several brands and compare them for quality. I did this and was surprised that there is quite a difference between brands.

Manufacturers often advertise that their extracts are made from the finest quality Bourbon beans. The term "Bourbon" bean simply means that the beans used in the extracts came from Madagascar, Comoro Islands, or Reunion. The beans are from the *Vanilla planifolia* stock which originally came from Mexico. The name comes from the island of Reunion which was formerly called Bourbon and which was the first island planted with the beans.

Keep vanilla extract tightly bottled in a cool dark place. Like good whiskey, vanilla benefits from aging, but loses some of its potency when consistently exposed to heat or bright light.

One last comment. If you find that you use pure vanilla extract frequently, you may want to purchase it in bulk. Like many food products, vanilla is cheaper in larger quantities. Some specialty food stores carry 8-ounce containers. If you can't easily find it in bulk, check the directory and contact one of the places for information.

CHOOSING VANILLA BEANS

Most suppliers that carry vanilla beans get them from Madagascar, Comoro Islands, or Reunion. Some also carry Tahitian and Mexican beans. If you purchase beans from a reliable source such as from one of the distributors listed in the directory, you will get good quality beans.

Top quality Mexican vanilla beans are considered by *most* experts as the best available anywhere. They have thin skins, a moisture level of about 25% (compared to Bourbons at 20% and Javas at 15% or lower), and are flexible. The difficulty is that they aren't often available. Top quality Bourbon beans are excellent, and the differences between them and Mexican beans are nominal.

On the other hand, vanilla beans from Tahiti are quite different. The Tahitian beans are fatter than Mexican or Bourbon beans. This is partly due to a high moisture level. Their skin is thicker than the other beans, the centers viscous, and they have less seeds than the Mexican and Madagascar beans. But their vanillin content is not as high as the others and as a consequence they are not as flavorful. The beans imported from Bali are dry and brittle and very low in vanillin content. They are primarily used in extracts, and are not really suitable for home use.

Vanilla beans can be stored in an airtight bottle, in alcohol (see page 25), or in sugar. If the purchased beans are too dry or hard, place a half of a small potato into the container with the beans. This will soften them, Another technique is to soak the bean in warm water or milk for a few minutes. This will make the bean more pliable and easier to cut open.

SYNTHETICS AND BLENDS

As vanilla has always been an expensive commodity, there have been many attempts to create substitutes and synthetics. The first synthetic vanilin placed on the market was made by German chemists in 1874 from *coniferin*, the glucoside that makes some pine trees smell like vanilla. In 1891, a French chemist, De Taire, ex-

The author wishes to thank Benjamin H. Kaestner, III, Director of Spice Procurement, and McCormick & Co., Inc.,—the world's largest marketer of pure vanilla products— for the photographs used in this book.

THE VANILLA
S T O R Y

The curing process for vanilla beans can take up to five months. Starting with a freshly harvested green pod (far left), it is eventually dried to the thin vanilla bean ready for use (far right).

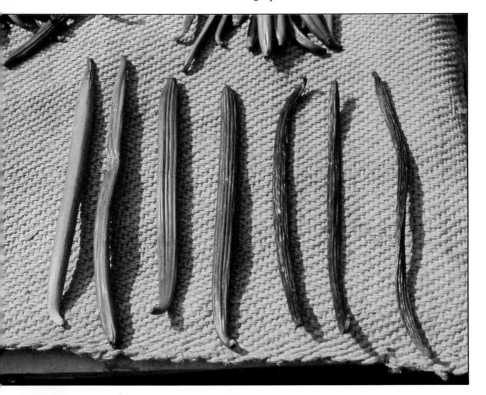

Vanilla beans emerge from pollinated orchid blossoms. The vanilla orchid blooms in the morning, begins to wilt by early afternoon, and is completely wilted by evening if it has not been pollinated.

About one meter in height, a fresh vanilla cutting is trained up its tutor tree. Three years will pass before the first blossoms appear. Left on its own, a vine can grow to the top of the jungle canopy—as high as 100 feet above the jungle floor.

Taking a break from the intense labor of vanilla cultivation, a worker stands beside a vanilla vine that has been "looped" on the tutor tree. By creating long, looped drapes of vanilla vines, the blossoms are brought within arm's length for pollination.

A Totonaca Indian worker hand pollinates the vanilla orchid in Mexico, using the traditional stylus.

In 1841, Edmund Albius—an ex-slave from the island of Reunion—re-discovered this technique of hand pollination.

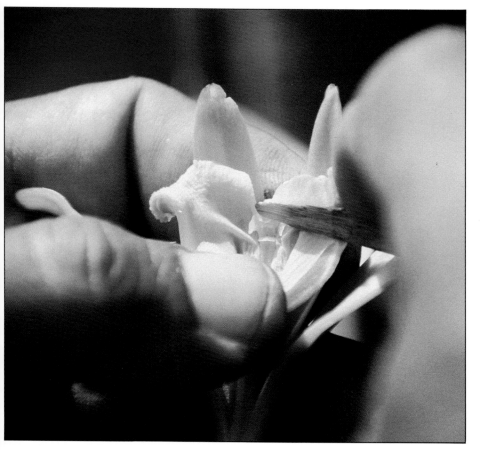

Clusters of vanilla beans mature for eight months before ready to harvest. Such a lengthy maturation can lead to problems of theft by vanilla rustlers. To protect their crops, some Madagascar owners brand each maturing pod with distinct insignias. The branding is done by cork-and-needle or by a signet ring.

In Mexico, vanilla beans are sometimes "killed" in slow ovens (thus halting the enzymatic growth process). Beans are laid in wooden boxes and placed in the ovens.

In Madagascar, before drying vanilla beans in the sun, the beans are "killed" by blanching for 20 seconds in 190-degree water. Blanching also halts the enzymatic growth process.

After blanching, vanilla beans are steamed in boxes for several days.

The hot tropical sun is perfect for drying vanilla beans. Tended by native workers in Madagascar, the sun-curing process takes two to three months before the beans are removed for sorting later. At night, the beans are wrapped to maintain the heat.

After sweating, vanilla beans are carried to open fields to dry in the sun. Shown here are workers on the Comoro Islands preparing to lay the beans out to dry.

After sun-curing, the beans are laid out for sorting and grading. The very best and largest beans are left to be used whole. Short or split beans can be used in preparation of vanilla extract.

Beans are also dried on racks above ground.

Bundles of cured vanilla beans packed for shipment create a striking pattern. The entire cultivation process—from planting to market—has taken approximately five to six years, one of the reasons for vanilla's precious value.

When ready for market, the beans are bundled for shipment. Shown here is a Mexican worker bundling the finished, cured beans.

"Mi Oficina" bar, scene of numerous vanilla negotiations, Gutierrez, Zamora, Mexico.

tracted vanillin from *eugonol,* which occurs in the oil of cloves. It was sold on the market at $12 an ounce and was used as commercial "vanillin" for a long time. The current synthetic vanillin is made from coal tar or the by-product of wood pulp. This by-product is sulphite liquor, an effluent from pulp paper making.

The Ontario Paper Company claims to be the world's largest producer of artificial vanillin. Actually, this was one of the first ecological solutions in the 1930's. The sulphite effluent is not biodegradable and was polluting local streams. Artificial vanillin was developed as part of the search to find positive uses for the effluent.

Vanillin is chemically pure, but the flavor doesn't come close to matching the flavor of true vanilla extract. This is in part because vanillin is only one component of the flavors in vanilla, or about 30% of the taste. *Piperonal,* for instance, is a crucial constituent for the unique perfume and flavor of vanilla, but it is not part of vanillin.

A major problem in using synthetic vanillas, or blends, is that there is no set standard for strength. It may be the same strength as *pure* extracts or it may be ten times as strong. Some imitation vanillas have a stronger odor than pure extracts and a much stronger taste with a somewhat unpleasant aftertaste. Some imitations —the ones made from the wood pulp effluent—tend to have a slight smell of wood about them rather like freshly cut pine. A simple taste test is to put some *pure vanilla extract* on a sugar cube and some *vanillin* on another. Taste the pure vanilla extract first as the vanillin will overpower the taste-buds. You will notice the difference in the flavors.

MEXICAN VANILLAS AND SYNTHETICS

Mexico is not producing enough vanilla for its own internal use today, so synthetics abound throughout the country. Because of the reputation for having the best vanilla anywhere, the manufacturers of synthetics use this to their advantage.

Mexico does not have the same labelling laws as in the United States. Virtually anything can be written on the labels. My mother returned from Mexico recently with a "vanilla" product manufactured in Guadalajara. The copy tells about how Mexican vanilla is un-excelled throughout the world for quality, taste, and fragrance. The two-bottle packet contains one bottle of "red vanilla" and one of "cristal vanilla." The red vanilla is supposedly from the whole bean and the cristal vanilla is made from the juices pressed from the bean so that puddings and ice creams won't be discolored—or so the label tells us.

My mother had in fact purchased a synthetic *vanillin* made from wood pulp effluent, and possibly with coumarin as a booster. The "cristal vanilla" was pure vanillin. Nothing on any of the labels gave an indication that the product was synthetic. Unfortunately, this is true with much "vanilla" from Mexico.

There are a few ways to determine if the vanilla in question is pure or synthetic. The major determinant is whether or not the product contains alcohol. If it is pure vanilla extract it will be high in alcohol content. Most synthetics contain no alcohol; a few contain 2% alcohol.

Price is another factor. The synthetics will be very inexpensive. Pure vanilla extract will be close in price to our extracts.

Determining pure vanilla by color or smell alone is difficult for the inexperienced buyer. Some synthetics will look dark and muddy, but synthetic vanilla made from coumarin may be the same color as the pure extract. The smell of vanillin is quite strong but also very "familiar." The pure extract will have a more subtle smell.

The wisest decision would be to avoid buying vanilla in Mexico unless you are in the company of someone who knows the differences between the pure and the synthetics. Pure vanilla extract from Mexico can be purchased in the United States. Check the directory for the distributor (pages 20, 21).

USING PURE VANILLA EXTRACTS AND VANILLA BEANS

Pure vanilla extract has a number of qualities that have not been widely publicized. Besides being a delightful flavoring, it can act as a "lifter," as with chocolate which tends to be somewhat flat by itself. The Aztecs "married" these two luxury items for that very reason. The chocolate industry would suffer greatly without pure or synthetic vanilla.

Vanilla also highlights meats, vegetables, and fruits. It softens and blends egg mixtures, takes the acidic bite out of acid foods—such as lemons—and accentuates the sweetness in fruits or baked goods. Custards and creams benefit from the perfumed quality of vanilla, especially if the bean is used. Vanilla can be used successfullly in savory foods, as well as foods traditionally associated with vanilla.

Vanilla beans can be used repeatedly in creams and stocks. After using the bean, wipe it off and put it away until you are ready to use it again. The beans tend to lose their strength after being used with chocolate, however.

Many of the recipes in this book call for the vanilla bean to be split open, and frequently to have the seeds scraped out of the bean. Here's how to slice open the bean *without* slicing open your fingers:

1. Make a small cut into the bean, about 3/4 of an inch from the tip.
2. Place finger on the tip of the bean, slip the knife point into the small incision, and slice the bean open lengthwise, cutting away from the fingers.
3. Open the vanilla bean, laying the sides flat to the table, and scrape out the seeds.

Most likely you have heard about vanilla sugar, and perhaps you make it already. If not, here's how:

VANILLA SUGAR

There are a number of recipes for making vanilla sugar. The simplest is to place whole or split vanilla beans into a jar of granulated or confectioners sugar. Seal the lid tightly and allow the beans to remain at least one week before using the sugar. Shake the jar once or twice a day to circulate sugar. This method will produce a fragrant sugar, but with minimal vanilla flavor.

To make a more richly flavored vanilla sugar, use one of the following two techniques:

1. Split a vanilla bean in half, then scrape the seeds of the two halves into 3 cups of granulated sugar, or 1 box of confectioners sugar. Place the vanilla sugar into a jar with a good seal. Add the sliced pieces of the bean, then close tightly. The sugar will be flavorful in about 1 day and will continue to grow in flavor over the next week.
2. The other technique is to put sugar into a blender or food processor.

For each cup of sugar, use approximately 2 inches of the vanilla bean, split in half and cut into small pieces. Whirl through the blender or pulse in food processor until the pieces of bean have been pulverized. Store as above. Before using sugar treated this way, pour it through a sieve.

Beans that are used to flavor custards or other liquids (except for chocolate) can be stored in the sugar jars. This will keep the beans well protected and will add additional fragrance to the sugar.

Beans stored in sugar will keep indefinitely, but the fragrance will slowly wear away with time. The beans will probably need replacing within a year or so. Beans used to flavor liquids will lose their flavor and scent more rapidly.

VANILLA COOKING OIL

A delicately perfumed and flavored oil can be made for cooking and as a salad oil. Place a vanilla bean that has been split open into a pint of good quality oil. Allow the bean to remain in the oil. Within a week the oil will be flavored. Add additional oil to the container as needed.

NOTED WITH INTEREST

As strange as it may seem to have so many grades of vanilla and to have synthetics made from such odd sources as wood pulp, at least quality extracts and beans are available and affordable. In earlier times this wasn't so, as exemplified by Balzac in *La Rabouilleuse* when he spoke of a vanilla substitute in, "...little pots of cream in which the vanilla had been replaced by burnt oats, as much like vanilla as chicory is like coffee."

GLOSSARY OF TERMS FOR PURE AND SYNTHETIC VANILLAS

PURE VANILLA EXTRACT:
Amber-colored liquid made from vanilla beans, alcohol and water. May contain sugar. Must contain at least 35% alcohol, and is the extractive of 13.35 oz. of vanilla beans.

VANILLA FLAVOR:
A mix of pure vanilla extract and synthetic substances, most commonly, vanillin.

NATURAL VANILLA FLAVOR:
A mix of pure vanilla extract and other natural substances extracted from natural sources other than the vanilla bean.

IMITATION VANILLA:
A mixture made from synthetic substances which imitate the pure vanilla extract smell and flavor.

ARTIFICIAL VANILLIN (Lignin Vanillin):
An artificial by-product of the paper industry, chemically treated to resemble the taste of pure vanilla extract. Used in vanilla flavor and imitation vanilla. But the taste is not like pure vanilla extract.

NATURAL VANILLIN:
The natural substance found in the vanilla bean. It is not a synthetic. Products labelled "vanillin" *are* synthetic.

ETHYL VANILLIN:
An ingredient sometimes used in imitation vanilla which is three times as strong as artificial vanillin and is a coal tar derivative.

COUMARIN:
A derivative of the tonka bean, often used in synthetic Mexican vanillas.

COOKIE VANILLA:
A pure vanilla extract made from a blend of Tahitian and Madagascar vanilla beans which the Cook Flavoring Company says is ideal for making

cookies. Cook also makes a pure vanilla extract from just Madagascar beans which they claim is not as sweet.

ESSENTIAL OIL OF VANILLA

Essential oils are highly concentrated essences in an oil base. There is a natural vanilla oil called "Vanilla Absolute" which is available but almost prohibitively expensive. Unfortunately, all of the vanilla essential oils on the market are made with artifician vanillin. They do, however, have a pleasant smell. Vanilla extract can be substituted for essential oils in most cases. I experimented with it, and it worked well, though the fragrance of the oil does last longer. Whether using the extract or the essential oil, here are a few ideas for bringing the fragrance of vanilla into your home.

Scented Lamp Oil

Experiment to determine just how strong you will want the vanilla smell emanating from your oil lamp. Begin with 10 to 15 drops to every quart of lamp oil.

Natural Room Fresheners

Rub a few drops of pure vanilla extract or essential oil on a light bulb for a quick release of vanilla into the room. It works very much like incense without the smoke.

Put a few drops of oil on paper vacuum cleaner bags. When the vacuum is running, the vanilla scent will fill the room.

Scenting Candles

Whether the candles are made professionally or at home from melted down candles, they will benefit with a little vanilla essence. Or place some oil on purchased candles. This is especially nice in the kitchen.

Massage Oil

Massage oils can be made from any quality vegetable or nut oils. I use a blend of 1 part sweet almond oil, 1 part apricot oil, and 3 parts olive oil. I like the texture of this mixture, but others work well too. Add about 1 tablespoon of pure vanilla extract or a few drops of the essential oil of vanilla to a pint of oil. A vanilla bean can also be placed in the oil; this will accentuate the bouquet.

Keep massage oils in the refrigerator until ready to use to prevent the oils from becoming rancid. Warm the oil for a few minutes in a bowl of warm water or allow the oil to come to room temperature before using.

DIRECTORY FOR VANILLA PRODUCTS

For the past five years I have been a distributor of Tahitian Import / Export, Inc. vanilla, the vanilla I consider to be the best available. You can place wholesale or retail orders through me by contacting:
Patricia Rain
116 Forest Avenue
Santa Cruz, CA 95062

You can also order directly from:
Tahitian Import / Export, Inc.
P. O. Box 35327
Los Angeles, CA 90035.

Cook's vanilla, another premium-quality vanilla extract, can be purchased in most gourmet markets or order directly:
COOKS FLAVORING COMPANY
200 Sherwood Road
Paso Robles, CA 93446

For essential oil of vanilla, contact:
Auracacia
P. O. Box 3157
Santa Rosa, CA 95402
(Artificial vanillin is used in their oils, but the quality of oil is good. If interested, inquire about "Vanilla Absolute" which is a pure vanilla oil.)

Vanilla Planifolia Cuttings

Stewart Orchids
P.O. Box 550
Carpenteria, CA 93013

Orchids by Haysermann
P.O. Box 363
Elmhurst, Il 60126

Oak Hill Gardens
P.O. Box 25, Binnie Road
Dundee, IL 60118

Santa Barbara Orchid Estate
1250 Orchid Drive
Santa Barbara, CA 93111

American Orchid Society, Inc.
6000 South Olive Avenue
West Palm Beach, FL 33405
305 / 585-8666
(This address is for anyone interested
in becoming a member of the organi-
zation, who needs further assistance
in locating Vanilla planifolia cuttings,
or who wants to order The Orchids:
A Scientific Survey, edited by Carl L.
Withner, published 1959, Ronald Press.)

In the early 1980s, Marc Jones was a sous chef at the Bel Air Sands in Los Angeles. His mother, Manina, had moved to Tahiti recently, and knowing her son loved to cook, she sent him some Tahitian vanilla beans. The beans smelled and looked so superior to the beans he'd used in the past that he decided to show the chefs he worked with. They experimented with the beans, were thrilled with their results, and Marc placed his first order.

Shortly afterwards, Marc told his friend, Peter Stone, about his exciting new business. Peter, who was at that time in the jewelry business, said he would be interested in marketing and selling beans. His endeavors were immediately successful, so the two men set up a partnership with Marc moving to Tahiti in order to guarantee production, and Peter primarily handling the marketing and sales stateside. In retrospect Peter says, "What a fantasy, to travel to exotic places, purchase a valuable product, and be part of the international import market."

GROWING YOUR OWN

Although anyone living north of Florida would be facing an uphill struggle to grow vanilla vines commercially, it is not difficult to grow the vines, flowers—and even the beans—on a small scale at home, given the proper conditions.

A greenhouse environment or a protected patio would provide a good home for the vines. Even an office or home will work, provided the room is reasonably humid and gets adequate light. The temperatures should not fall below 55 to 60 degrees farenheit.

There is a listing in the directory of four places where *Vanilla planifolia* vines can be ordered (see page 21).

Once you have a cutting, take a large clay pot, soak it for a few minutes to dampen the terra cotta, and place pieces of a broken pot in the bottom of the pot for drainage. Set the rooted vanilla plant along with a wooden pole or tree fern log (for support) into the pot. Fill the pot with a terrestrial mix consisting of equal parts of loam, sharp sand, and peat. Place gravel on top of the soil to secure the plant and support. Then attach the stem in several places to the vertical support.

Once the vine becomes established on the support, you may wish to train the vine along a trellis. This is not only attractive, but the vines flower and fruit better when grown like this. Apparently bending the vine produces flowers and fruits beyond the bend.

The humidity should be high. Although vanilla plants like bright light, they should be shaded in the summer if it is hot. Filtered light is ideal.

The plant will not flower for quite some time, possibly up to 3 years. This will give you ample time, however, to figure out how to hand-pollinate the flowers so that your plant will produce fruits.

As I have never personally seen the flowers being hand-pollinated, I would prefer to refer you to a good book for more detailed information on how to grow the vanilla vines, than to tackle the diagrams and techniques myself.

There is a comprehensive chapter on the history, commerce, and biology of *Vanilla planifolia*, titled "Vanilla —The Orchid of Commerce," in *The Orchids: A Scientific Survey*, edited by Carl L. Withner and published in 1959 by Ronald Press. Mr. Withner was an associate professor of biology at Brooklyn College and the resident investigator of orchids at the Brooklyn Botanic Garden, and as such, is far more qualified than I on advising you of the idiosyncracies of orchids. It is a good chapter, though somewhat technical, and it will give you all the information you will need for your undertaking. This book can be ordered from The American Orchid Society as well as from booksellers who advertise in The American Orchid Society monthly bulletin.

If orchids interest you—and being the largest family of flowering plants the world, there are probably a few in plants at the very least that will catch your fancy—it might be worthwhile to become a member of the American Orchid Society. Their address is:

American Orchid Society, Inc.
6000 South Olive Avenue
West Palm Beach, Florida 33405
(305) 585-8666

If indeed you do decide to grow the vanilla vines, please let me know how you fare. When I have the opportunity to have a good greenhouse I would like to give it a go...I can't imagine a more exotic plant hobby than growing tropical plants in a temperate climate. Write to me in care of my publisher: Patricia Rain, c/o Celestial Arts, P.O. Box 7327, Berkeley, CA 94707.

VANILLA RECIPES

1
EXTRACTS, LIQUEURS & BEVERAGES

Vanilla is used in a number of commercial drinks and liqueurs. Although the actual amount may be small, its presence helps to enhance the other flavors. It acts as a "lifter," balancing heavy flavors as well as imparting its own delicate flavor and fragrance. Recipes for several liqueurs that can be made at home follow, as well as extracts and cordials that can be used to enhance beverages of baked goods and custards.

Beverages also benefit from the addition of vanilla extract. Fruit drinks containing peaches, apricots, berries, apples, and citrus, and of course, milk-based drinks, are enhanced by the use of vanilla.

Making vanilla extract is quite simple, and the flavor imparted is often richer in character than the commercial extracts. Bert Greene in his charming book *Kitchen Bouquets,* published by Simon and Schuster, has a section devoted to vanilla. In it he tells how he stores his vanilla beans:

I keep my vanilla bean in an old apothecary bottle with a tight, ground-glass stopper. More to the point, after I place the vanilla bean inside the glass container, I pour in enough cognac or 100 proof vodka to immerse the pod completely in liquid. Within a month or so, the alcohol takes on a deep amberlike hue and its aroma can knock your hat off. It is the purest infusion of golden vanilla you have ever sniffed.

This kind of distilled flavoring is most desirable when recipes call for large measures of liquid vanilla. When the alcohol starts to run low, I merely add a few drams to the original concoction and keep pouring away.

Brillat Savarin, in his treatise on chocolate in the Physiology of Taste, *says, "And when we add the delicious perfume of vanilla to this mixture of sugar, cacao and cinnamon, we achieve the ne plus ultra of perfection, to which such a concoction may be carried."*

This is the recipe that I have used for extract and also as a base for a cordial that can be used as an extract as well.

VANILLA EXTRACT

Place 6 *long beans,* split open and cut into pieces into *1 quart of good quality vodka.* Cap tightly and place in a cool dark place. Leave for 1 month to 6 weeks, shaking the bottle occasionally.

Before using, sieve through a strainer lined with cheesecloth (or use a coffee filter), rinse the bottle to remove residue, and pour back into the bottle. Add one whole vanilla bean and cap tightly until used.

•

VANILLA CORDIAL

Make the extract according to the previous recipe. After straining the extract, place the beans into a medium saucepan. Add *1 cup sugar* and *1/2 cup water.* Bring to a boil, stirring constantly. Continue to boil about 3 minutes more, stirring occasionally.

Pour the syrup through the sieve lined with fresh cheesecloth into the extract. Sieve again back into the bottle. There will be come extra cordial which should be placed into another container (or perhaps used right away so not to waste it!). The cordial will be better if allowed to mellow for at least 1 week. Use it as a flavoring or as a late afternoon or after dinner liqueur. It tastes somewhat like Tuaca but has a much stronger vanilla flavor.

•

Tlilxochitl, the word the Aztecs used for vanilla, was derived from "Tlilli" meaning "black," and xochitl," now interpreted as meaning pod. In a thesaurus written in 1651 by Hernandez, however, the word was interpreted as "black flowers." This fallacy about the color of the vanilla orchid continued for many years in Europe; it wasn't until the orchids actually flowered in Europe that many people who were familiar with vanilla discovered that the flowers were greenish-yellow.

Another recipe for making extract with brandy, was given to me by a friend:

BRANDY VANILLA EXTRACT

8 plump vanilla beans
4 cups good brandy

Split each bean lengthwise down the center to expose the tiny seeds. Place the beans in a jar deep enough to contain the vanilla beans without bending them. Pour in the brandy. Cover tightly and let the flavors mingle for about 4 weeks, storing on a cool, dark shelf. Shake the bottle often.

If decanting for gifts, place 2 beans per container, pour the brandy over, and cover tightly.

•

In Maida Heatter's *New Book of Great Desserts,* she has a recipe for Irish Cream Liqueur which she had apparently been saving to use in an appropriate book. She finally decided to put it in this book, but as there was no section that was really appropriate for the liqueur, she put it into the introduction.

Fortunately, it is easily assimilated into this book; it is an excellent substitute for the commercial liqueur.

HOMEMADE IRISH CREAM LIQUEUR

1 cup Irish whiskey
1 14-ounce can sweetened
  condensed milk
4 eggs
2 tablespoons pure vanilla extract
2 tablespoons chocolate extract
1 tablespoon coconut extract
1 tablespoon powdered instant
  espresso or other powdered
  (not granular) instant coffee

In a blender, blend all the ingredients at low speed until thoroughly mixed. Transfer to a bottle with a tight cover and refrigerate overnight or longer. Serve very cold. Shake well before serving.

•

Karen Delee is the postmistress in the small town near where I live. She and her assistants have helped me jam manuscripts and stories into mailing envelopes and have searched for zip codes for me when the rural mail pick-up truck was due any minute. I appreciate Karen far more than I'm sure she appreciates me. She did, however, take quite an interest in this book as she has organized and participated in local fairs where many of our talented residents sell their crafts, books, and foods. She and her friend, Marilynn, have a coffee liqueur recipe which she offered for this book.

KAREN AND MARILYNN'S HOMESTYLE KAHLUA

4 cups sugar
4 cups water
1/2 cup instant coffee
1 whole vanilla bean cut up into
small pieces
1 quart vodka

Mix the sugar and water in a large, non-aluminum pot. Add the coffee and vanilla bean, cut into pieces, and bring to a simmer. Keep at a low simmer for 45 minutes. Remove from stove and cool completely. Add 1 quart vodka.

Strain mixture and pour into dark bottles. Let sit in a cool dark place for 3 weeks before using.

•

This is a recipe that I have had for years. I don't remember where it came from. It is quite strong and sweet and is good as a liqueur, over ice cream, or for flavoring other drinks. Chocolate could be added to it as well for a coffee-chocolate liqueur.

VANILLA COFFEE LIQUEUR

4 cups sugar
1 cup instant coffee powder
2 vanilla beans, split open
1 cup boiling water
3 cups brandy or bourbon

Mix together the sugar and instant coffee powder. Pour the boiling water over the coffee and sugar, and stir until all ingredients are well dissolved and blended. Place the vanilla beans into a bottle, pour in coffee mixture, and add brandy or bourbon. Age at least 30 days in a cool, dark place, turning and shaking the bottle gently every few days.

•

Marshall Neale, Director of the Vanilla Information Bureau, responded with enthusiasm to a letter I sent asking for information on vanilla. He graciously complied to help me as I sent chapter after chapter of this book to check for accuracy and additional information. In one of his return packets he sent along these 2 liqueur recipes which had been produced in the test kitchens of his company.

VANILLA ORANGE LIQUEUR

1 cup water
1-1/4 cups sugar
Thin orange peelings from 1 large
    orange
1 vanilla bean, split lengthwise or
    4 teaspoons pure vanilla extract
3 tablespoons pure orange extract
1 teaspoon pure lemon extract
8 drops yellow food coloring
    (optional)
1 drop red food coloring (optional)
2 cups (90 to 100 proof) vodka

In a medium saucepan combine
water, sugar, orange peelings, and
vanilla bean. Bring to boiling point.
Boil, uncovered, for 5 minutes, stirring
occasionally. Remove from heat; stir
in orange and lemon extracts and
food colorings. Cool. Add vodka.
Pour into jars with tight fitting covers.
Let stand 2 weeks before serving.
Makes 1 quart.

VANILLA-ANISE LIQUEUR

2-1/2 cups sugar
1-1/2 cups water
4 teaspoons pure vanilla extract
4 teaspoons pineapple extract
1-1/2 teaspoons pure anise extract
1/2 teaspoon pure banana extract
1 bottle (fifth) vodka

In a small saucepan bring sugar
and water to boil; boil 5 minutes.
Remove from heat and stir in extracts.
Cool thoroughly. In a large pitcher
combine syrup with vodka; blend
well. Stir in a few drops of yellow food
coloring if desired. Store in a tightly
covered bottle. Makes 5-2/3 cups.

The following recipe for eggnog is
extremely rich. It is perfectly reasonable to use just rum or brandy, to
lower the alcohol content, or to make
it without alcohol. One way to serve
eggnog at a family party is to have
decanters of rum and brandy next
to the eggnog bowl.

VANILLA EGGNOG

12 large eggs, separated, the whites
    at room temperature
2 cups sugar
3 tablespoons vanilla
2 cups brandy
1 cup dark rum
4 cups milk. (If making without alcohol,
    add 1 to 2 cups more milk)
2 cups well chilled heavy cream
freshly grated nutmeg to taste

In a large bowl, beat egg yolks using
an electric mixer or whip, until they are
pale. Beat in the sugar, a little at a
time, and beat mixture until it is thick
and pale. Whisk in the vanilla, brandy,
rum and milk.

In another large bowl beat the egg
whites with a pinch of cream of tarter
until they hold soft peaks, and fold
them into the yolk mixture gently but
thoroughly. In another bowl beat the
cream until it holds soft peaks and
fold it into the yolk mixture. Chill the
eggnog for at least 3 hours and up
to 5 hours.

Before serving, stir gently and
sprinkle with nutmeg. Makes about
16 cups.

HOT BUTTERED RUM AND CIDER

For each drink, use:
1 inch strip of orange peel
2 inch piece of vanilla bean
1 to 1-1/2 jiggers golden or dark rum

1 generous teaspoon unsalted butter
1 small piece cinnamon stick
3 pinches each powdered cloves and allspice
1 cup scalding hot cider

Heat spices, vanilla bean, and orange peel in apple cider. Place rum and butter into mugs. Pour cider into mugs, straining out spices if preferred.

•

During the long, wet winters on the coast of California, we often serve hot rum and tea. It is essentially the same as the rum and cider except that water is used instead of cider, and either herbal or black tea is used.

RUM AND TEA

Place the spices and tea into a teapot. Pour boiling water over and allow to steep for about 5 minutes. Add to rum and butter in mugs, and sweeten to taste with maple syrup or brown sugar if desired.

•

While working on this book, I asked a local bartender if I could taste **Tuaca**, an Italian vanilla liqueur. Although it is quite sweet, it has a pleasant underlying flavor of both vanilla and orange. The bartender gave me two recipes that he makes using Tuaca, though a number of people drink it straight or over ice. Later, in a liquor store, I read the label on the bottle which said that Tuaca came from a secret Italian recipe first made over 500 years ago. I found that interesting, as vanilla wasn't introduced to Europe until the 1500's and wasn't readily available until the 1600's. But then, who am I to argue with secrets and legends? A little mystery is always good for the imagination...

ITALIAN COFFEE

In a *cup of hot* coffee or *espresso*, add *one shot of Tuaca* and top with *whipped cream.*

•

HOT APPLE PIE

For each serving use:

1 cup apple cider
1 shot of Tuaca
2 cloves
1 cinnamon stick
1 vanilla bean
whipped cream garnish

Heat cider with cloves, cinnamon, and vanilla bean (use the same amount of spices for up to 4 servings. The spices can also be used again. If making a large amount of cider, double the spices).

When hot, pour into cups, add Tuaca, and garnish with whipped cream.

•

APPLE HUMMER

For each serving:

1-1/2 ounces Apple Schnapps
1 ounce white rum
1 scoop vanilla ice cream
1 teaspoon pure vanilla extract
small amount of crushed ice

Blend the ingredients until creamy. Serve in a chilled glass.

•

RAZ-MA-TAZZ

2-1/2 cups softened French vanilla
*   ice cream*
2-1/2 ounces raspberry liqueur
1-1/2 ounces brandy
1 teaspoon pure vanilla extract
fresh raspberries for garnish

Blend ice cream, liqueur, brandy, and extract until creamy. Pour into chilled glasses and garnish with fresh raspberries. Strawberries could be substituted for raspberries if desired. Serves 4.

•

MILK PUNCH

For each serving:

3 ounces half-and-half
1 teaspoon confectioners sugar
1-1/4 ounces bourbon
1/2 teaspoon pure vanilla extract
Nutmeg (garnish)

Heat half-and-half and sugar in small saucepan until almost boiling, stirring frequently. Combine with bourbon and vanilla. Mix well. Pour into warmed cup and top with nutmeg.

This same recipe can be run through the blender instead of being heated. Add a small handful of crushed ice to the blender, and serve in chilled glasses.

•

PIÑA VAINILLA COLADA

7 cups crushed ice
3 cups cubed fresh pineapple
2-3/4 cups pineapple juice
1 15-ounce can cream of coconut
1/4 cup half and half
2 teaspoons pure vanilla extract
1-1/2 cups 151-proof rum
*   (heavy dark rum)*
3 to 4 ounces rum (added to
*   glasses last)*

Mix the first 6 ingredients in a blender in batches, mixing thoroughly, about 3 minutes. Add rum and blend 1 minute longer. Serve colada in chilled glasses. Top each with 1/2 oz rum. Serves 6 to 8.

•

CAROLINA SPICED TEA

8 cups water
8 cloves
1 cinnamon stick
1 vanilla bean
3-inch piece lemon peel
5-inch piece orange peel
4 tea bags
1 6-ounce can frozen orange juice
   concentrate
1/2 cup sugar
2 lemons

Combine first 6 ingredients and bring to a boil. Add 4 teabags and steep 20 minutes. Remove peels and spices and add juice of lemons, orange juice concentrate and sugar (or to taste). Serve hot or cold. Add rum if desired.

●

GLÖGG

7 cardamom pods
20 cloves
4 sticks cinnamon
2 vanilla beans, split open, seeds
   scraped out
1 cup sugar
2 bottles red wine
1 pint aquavit or colorless fruit
   brandy
3-1/2 ounces currants
3-12 ounces blanched almonds

Place spices, vanilla, and sugar in a serving pot or punch bowl. Pour in wine and heat (or pour in heated wine), then add brandy and ignite.

Serve in glasses or mugs. Place almonds and currants on small plates as an accompaniment.

●

HOT SPICED WINE

1 quart dry red wine
1 cup sugar
1 cup water
1 teaspoon whole cloves
1 cinnamon stick
1 vanilla bean, split open
1 lemon, sliced
1/2 orange, sliced

Combine all ingredients in a large saucepan. Bring to boil over high heat, then simmer 15 minutes. Strain and serve hot. Serves about 10.

●

Using vanilla in non-alcoholic drinks can be as creative as you wish. The following recipes will give you some ideas for drinks, but experiment with your own drinks as well.

THREE FRUIT NECTAR

2 cups grapefruit juice
2 cups orange juice
1 cup pineapple juice
2 cups water
4 teaspoons pure vanilla extract
lemon or lime slices

Combine juices, water and vanilla extract; mix well, or run in blender with ice cubes. Serve over ice. Garnish with lemon or lime slices.

•

This recipe was inspired from the traditional Indian *lassi,* a refreshing drink for hot weather or as an accompaniment to spicy foods.

VANILLA COOLER

1 cup milk
15 whole cloves
15 cardamom pods
2 cinnamon sticks
1 vanilla bean, split
1 cup vanilla yogurt
1 tablespoon honey
cracked ice cubes

Place milk and spices in a medium-sized saucepan. Scrape vanilla seeds into milk, and bring to scalding. Remove from the heat and let cool, then refrigerate until chilled. Strain into a blender; discard the spices. Add 1 cup vanilla yogurt and 1 tablespoon honey and blend until smooth. Cover the blender and refrigerate until ready to use. Just before serving, add 3 or 4 cracked ice cubes per serving to the blender and blend until frothy. Serves 2.

Despite its reputation as being bland or generic, vanilla is something which people feel strongly, even passionately, about. This is especially true of its fragrance. People regularly tell me how much they love the scent of vanilla and that they have chosen a particular perfume or fragrance based on its strong vanilla overtones. Some people even go directly to the source, using straight vanilla extract as a perfume.

Vanilla as a perfume is not just an aesthetic preference; those who wear it often feel it has strong aphrodisiacal qualities. The most amusing rationale behind this belief that I've heard came from a woman who said, "Men love the smell of vanilla because it reminds them of kitchens and baking. When they smell vanilla they associate it with food and comfort and they can't help but be attracted to the source."

This is a perfect drink for teens, a recipe that will bring back memories of soda fountains and dates, and wonderful sodas.

CHOCOLATE AND VANILLA CREAM SODA

3/4 cup chocolate syrup
2/3 cup half-and-half
dark chocolate ice cream
2 teaspoons pure vanilla extract
iced soda water
French vanilla ice cream

Place chocolate syrup, half and half, vanilla, and 1 large scoop of chocolate ice cream in a blender and blend 1 minute. Divide the mixture between 2 chilled glasses.

Add approximately 2/3 cup soda water to each glass and stir briskly with a spoon. Drop 2 large scoops vanilla ice cream into each glass, then top off the glasses with soda water. Drink quickly to keep froth from spilling over.

●

A really good milkshake is a treat. Unfortunately, it isn't so easy to find a good milkshake in this day and age. The ice cream is often inferior in quality, flavored with synthetic vanilla, and overly sweetened. There is nothing wrong, however, with producing the best possible milkshakes at home.

This is the formula that I use for a great vanilla milkshake, along with some variations. The basic recipe serves 2 or more; some of the variations serve more.

THE BASIC VANILLA MILKSHAKE

1 cup rich milk
1 pint top-quality vanilla ice cream
*   or vanilla-honey ice cream*
4 teaspoons pure vanilla extract
cracked ice cubes (optional)

Blend ingredients in a blender or food processor, and serve in chilled glasses.

Variations and Additions:
1. For Malted, add 2 tablespoons malted milk powder.
2. For fruit shake, add 1 ripe banana, 1 pint fresh berries, 3 peeled and pitted peaches, 2 cherimoyas if you can find them—(The most delectable of tropical fruits), 1 cup chopped dates, etc.
3. For Chocolate shake, add 2/3 cup good quality chocolate syrup.
4. For extra richness, add 1 egg.

●

COFFEE FROST

1 cup strong coffee, warm or room
 temperature
4 teaspoons sugar
2 cups milk
2 tablespoons pure vanilla extract
1/2 pint vanilla ice cream, softened

Mix coffee with sugar and stir until
sugar is dissolved. Chill. Add milk
and vanilla extract. Add ice cream;
run through blender until smooth.
(Add a couple of ice cubes to
blender, if desired.)

•

HOT MOCHA

3 tablespoons sugar
2 tablespoons unsweetened cocoa
2 teaspoons instant coffee powder
 (espresso powder would be best)
1/8 teapoon ground allspice
pinch salt
2 cups boiling water
2 cups scalded milk
1 tablespoon pure vanilla extract
vanilla whipped cream

In a small saucepan combine
sugar, cocoa, coffee, allspice, and
salt. Stir in 1/4 cup water; heat until
hot, stirring occasionally. Stir in vanilla
extract.
Serve in mugs topped with vanilla
whipped cream. Makes about 1
quart.

•

HOT CHOCOLATE MIX

3/4 cup granulated sugar
1/4 cup blanched almonds
1/2 cup unsweetened cocoa powder
1 vanilla bean, sliced open
1/2 teaspoon instant espresso coffee
 powder (optional)
1 teaspoon ground cinnamon
3.2 ounces dry nonfat milk,
 or enough to make 1 quart

Combine the sugar and almonds
in a blender or food processor, and
blend until it forms a smooth paste.
Split open vanilla bean, and scrape
seeds into mixture. Add cocoa, nonfat
dry milk, espresso, and cinnamon.
Process for 1 minute more. Store in
airtight container. This mix will keep
for several months and will make 2 to
4 cups, depending upon preferred
strength.

While anyone who loves hot chocolate would enjoy this gift in the winter,
it is an especially nice gift to give to
young people, either who live at
home or are out on their own. It's
a good package to take skiing or on
any chilly outdoor excursion, as well.

•

2
FRUITS & FRUIT DESSERTS

Vanilla enhances fruits by intensifying their flavors as well as highlighting their sweetness. Vanilla softens and neutralizes acid foods, so fruits that are naturally tart or acid, or fruits that are picked too green, benefit from the addition of a few drops of vanilla.

The next time you prepare fruit salad or fresh pineapple, divide the fruit into two separate bowls and add a little pure vanilla extract to one of the bowls. Mix it well and let the fruit absorb the vanilla for about ten minutes. Compare the two bowls of fruit. You will likely taste the difference. My daughter noticed the difference the addition of vanilla made in a winter salad which included raw pineapple that hadn't ripened evenly. Usually she turns away from pineapple because of the sore tongue caused by the acidity; this time she was fine.

The recipes in this chapter have been chosen to provide an unusual variety of ways to use fruit. Fruits are frequently interchangeable, so use what is available or in season.

When vanilla cuttings were taken to the island of Bourbon (now Reunion) in the mid 1800s, sugar cane was the principal crop. Vanilla became a highly esteemed cash crop very quickly, and almost all sugar plantations grew some vanilla as well. Indeed, the vine was so popular, that almost everyone, even the poorest inhabitants, covered their yards, porches, and other available spots with vanilla creepers.

FRESH FRUIT COMPOTE WITH VANILLA CREAM

1 cup water
1 cup sguar
1/2 cup fresh orange juice
1 navel orange (unpeeled), quartered
2 lemons (unpeeled), quartered
2 2-inch cinnamon sticks
8 whole cloves
1 tablespoon pure vanilla extract
1/4 teaspoon freshly grated nutmeg
2 ripe but firm pears, cored and sliced
3 large navel oranges, peeled and sliced
1 cup strawberries, sliced*
1/2 cup Muscat or other green grapes, halved and seeded
1/2 cup purple grapes, halved and seeded
1/2 cup red seedless grapes

*If this fruit compote is made during the winter and strawberries are unavailable, add slightly thawed blueberries or raspberries just before serving.

Combine water, sugar, orange juice, orange, lemons, cinnamon sticks, cloves, vanilla, and nutmeg in a non-aluminum 4-quart saucepan. Cook over low heat, stirring occasionally, until sugar dissolves. Increase heat and boil 5 minutes. Place pear slices in a large bowl. Strain hot syrup over pears. Cool to room temperature.

Gently stir sliced oranges, grapes, and berries into pears. Let stand at room temperature at least 1 hour. The compote can be made up to 2 days ahead, in the refrigerator, but allow to stand at room temperature for 1 hour before serving.

Spoon compote into bowls. Top each with a spoonful of vanilla cream.

●

VANILLA CREAM

3 ounces cream cheese, room
   temperature
3 tablespoons vanilla sugar
1 teaspoon pure vanilla extract
1 1-inch piece vanilla bean, split
   lengthwise
2/3 cup whipping cream.

Combine cream cheese, sugar, and vanilla in medium sized bowl. Scrape in seeds from vanilla bean. Mix until smooth, slowly adding whipping cream. Mix until fluffy and light. This can be made up to 3 days in advance and refrigerated.

●

The combination of cooking the pineapple briefly along with the addition of the vanilla bean in this recipe cuts the acidity down tremendously.

FRESH PINEAPPLE COMPOTE

1 medium-sized fresh pineapple
3/4 cup sugar
1-1/2 cups water
1 tablespoon lemon juice
dash salt
1 vanilla bean, split, or
1 tablespoon pure vanilla extract
2 tablespoons rum or Kirsch

Peel the pineapple, slice, and cut into wedges, removing the core. Set aside.

Combine sugar, water, lemon juice, salt, and vanilla bean in a saucepan, bring to the boiling point, and simmer 5 mintues. Add pineapple, cover, and cook 5 minutes or until pineapple is tender. Using a perforated spoon, remove pineapple from syrup.

Reduce syrup by one-fourth, and add rum or Kirsch and vanilla extract if vanilla bean was not used. Pour over pineapple, and allow to cool.

Serve as a dessert with vanilla cream sauce, vanilla chiffon sauce, or vanilla creme fraiche, or serve as an accompaniment to a meat dish. Serves about 6.

●

If the dried fruits being used are not very moist, soak them in hot English Breakfast tea or a heated fruit nectar or juice for 2 hours, then drain them very well. Proceed with recipe.

DRIED FRUIT COMPOTE WITH GINGER AND VANILLA

2 cups water or fruit juice
1 cup vanilla sugar (or less if using juice; sweeten to taste)
3/4 cup apple cider vinegar
2 3-inch cinnamon sticks
4 1/2-inch-thick pieces of fresh ginger, lightly smashed
1/2 teaspoon whole allspice berries
1 vanilla bean, split down the center
2 cups dried, but moist, fruits (peaches, pears, prunes, apricots, figs, etc.)

Place all ingredients except dried fruits in a 6-quart casserole. Place over low heat and cook mixture until the sugar has dissolved completely. When the sugar has dissolved, uncover the pot and bring the syrup to a boil; boil for 2 minutes.

Add dried fruits, cover casserole partially, leaving about 2 inches open at the top. Simmer the fruits for about 20 minutes, or until just tender. Remove the fruits and spices to a bowl with a slotted spoon.

Boil the syrup until it has condensed lightly, about 5 minutes, then strain syrup over fruits.

Let cool to room temperature, then cover and refrigerate. The fruits will keep in the refrigerator for several months.

Serve with *vanilla creme fraiche* or heavy cream.

●

FRESH GRAPES IN VANILLA AND CHAMPAGNE

3/4 cup natural to extra-dry champagne or sparkling wine
3/4 cup water
2/3 cup sugar
5 tablespoons lemon juice
1 full-bodied vanilla bean, split lengthwise
1 cup each green, red, and black seedless grapes (or all 1 color)
chilled champagne.

In large saucepan, combine the 3/4 cup champagne, water, sugar, lemon juice, and vanilla bean. Bring to a boil over high heat, stirring until sugar is dissolved. Boil until syrup is reduced to 1 cup.

Remove vanilla bean and scrape seeds into syrup. Add additional 1 teaspoon vanilla extract if desired. Cool syrup and refrigerate up to a week if being made ahead.

Add syrup and grapes to a medium-sized saucepan. Bring to boiling point on high heat. Boil just until grapes begin to soften and skins are just about to burst (about 3 minutes). Let cool, cover and chill for at least 3 hours.

Spoon grapes and champagne syrup into 6 champagne glasses. Splash in additional champagne and serve.

This recipe could be made with sparkling grape juice as long as juice is not too sweet. Reduce sugar to 1/3 to 1/2 cup if juice is sweet.

●

Jerry Goodman, who provided the inspiration for this book, has a recipe for poached pears in a cherry/raspberry sauce that is superb. The recipe evolved, Jerry says, from an original that called for currant juice, which he couldn't find in the stores, so he substituted cherry cider, which was available. He also substituted the raspberry liqueur for cassis which he also couldn't find. He misread the original recipe and combined the sauce ingredients with the poaching ingredients, cut out the extra sugar, and added cream at the end, and *voila!* This version is undoubtedly much better.

The poaching liquid will keep for several weeks in the refrigerator and can be reused several times. This is an excellent and colorful finale to a winter dinner as it is not cloyingly sweet.

JERRY GOODMAN'S WINE POACHED PEARS WITH RASPBERRY/CHERRY SAUCE

4 Comice, Packham, Bartlett, or
   Bosc pears, ripe, yet firm
1 bottle dry white wine
2 cups black cherry cider or juice
1 cup sugar
1 cinnamon stick
1 vanilla bean, split open but intact
zest of 1 lemon
2 tablespoons raspberry liqueur
1/2 cup heavy cream

Carefully peel the pears, leaving the stems intact.

In a deep saucepan combine the wine, cherry juice or cider, sugar, cinnamon stick, vanilla, and lemon zest and bring to a boil. Reduce heat to simmer and add the pears. The poaching liquid should completely cover the pears while cooking; add water or more wine if necessary.

Poach pears until tender, 25 to 35 minutes, and leave in the liquid until ready to serve.

Just before serving add raspberry liqueur. Serve warm or at room temperature with the pears standing upright in the serving dish, and poaching liquid spooned around them. Carefully add cream or pass separately.

●

Pears, like raspberries, go well with chocolate. This is a nice sophisticated sundae of sorts.

DANISH CHOCOLATE PEARS

1 quart water
1-1/2 cups vanilla sugar
1 vanilla bean, split
4 pears, peeled
4 ounces dark sweet chocolate
1/2 cup whipping cream
rich vanilla ice cream

Combine water, sugar and vanilla bean in a large saucepan, and bring to boil. Add the pears, reduce heat, and cook gently until tender, about 30 minutes, basting pears occasionally. Refrigerate pears in syrup for 24 hours.

Remove vanilla bean from syrup. Melt chocolate in heavy saucepan over low heat, stirring frequently until smooth and glossy. Scrape vanilla bean pulp into chocolate. Add cream and bring to boil, stirring constantly. Remove from heat.

To serve, place a scoop of ice cream in a dessert dish. Place pear alongside ice cream, and spoon chocolate sauce over top.

●

PAPILLOTE OF PEARS OR APPLES WITH ORANGE AND VANILLA

1 tablespoon melted butter
1 ripe pear, peeled, halved
  and cored, or
1 firm apple, peeled, halved
  and cored
2 teaspoons fresh lemon juice
1/2 vanilla bean, split open
1 tablespoon plus 1 teaspoon
  creme fraiche
2 teaspoons brown sugar or vanilla
  sugar
4 strips of orange zest, about
  2 inches long, and 1/2 inch wide
2 small scoops of vanilla ice cream
  or more creme fraiche

Preheat oven to 400 degrees. Fold two 15 by 20 inch pieces of parchment paper or aluminum foil in half crosswise.* Cut each rectangle into a heart shape with the fold running vertically down the center. Open up the hearts and brush each piece with 1/2 tablespoon of the butter.

Brush the pear or apple halves with lemon juice to prevent discoloration. Cut each half crosswise on the diagonal into 6 slices and place on half of each heart. Fan out.

Scrape the seeds from the vanilla bean and mix them with the *creme fraiche* and sugar. Spoon over pears or apples. Place strips of orange zest and pieces of the vanilla bean on top of fruits.

Fold the paper over the fruit. At the top of each heart, make a series of tight, overlapping folds to seal the papers.

Place the wrapped fruits on a cookie sheet and bake 12 minutes or until fruit is tender. Open at the table and serve at once with ice cream or *creme fraiche.*

This recipe is for 2 servings.

*Paper-wrapped foods impress people but appear to be difficult to prepare. It's really a simple technique and quite beneficial to the food as it holds in flavors and juices that normally evaporate in the oven.

•

PEACHES ANNETTE

2 cups water
3/4 cup sugar
1 vanilla bean, sliced lengthwise
6 firm ripe peaches, peeled

Make a light syrup by boiling water and sugar together for 5 minutes. Put peaches into a saucepan, pour syrup over them, and add vanilla bean. Bring the syrup to a boil and simmer gently for 10 to 15 minutes, or until peaches are tender. Cool peaches in syrup.

To serve, drain peaches from syrup, and serve with rich vanilla, almond, or coffee ice cream. Cover with kirsch-flavored *sauce riche.*

SAUCE RICHE:

1 cup heavy cream, whipped
1/2 cup vanilla sauce (see page 106)
1/4 cup kirschwasser (or other liqueur)

Fold whipped cream into vanilla sauce, and flavor with liqueur.

Other fruits such as pears, peaches, or pineapple, can be substituted for peaches if desired.

Firm varieties of peaches, especially some of the late-summer varieties, are ideal to use in this recipe. This is also a nice dessert for peaches that didn't get quite ripe enough to slice into cobbler or shortcake.

•

An elegant addition to homemade ice creams, cakes, puddings, and sweet yeastbreads when chopped.

APRICOTS IN APRICOT LIQUEUR

4 pounds dried apricots, either whole or in halves
4 vanilla beans
apricot liqueur or Schnapps

Lightly pack apricots into 1 large jar or 4 small jars. Slide vanilla bean(s) around apricots then cover with apricot liqueur or Schnapps. If the fruits are not real dry, about 3 cups of liqueur will be needed. If the fruits are dry, they can be soaked in apricot nectar or juice for a day before being packed in liqueur.

Let the apricots stand at room temperature for a few days, then refrigerate. They will keep for almost a year in the refrigerator, and will become more flavorful over time.

Peaches or pears can be substituted for apricots; use the appropriate liqueur for the fruit.

•

A good chutney is as colorful as it is delicious; this recipe is unusually attractive. Chutneys make a pungent accompaniment to hot or cold meats and poultry, and are an essential condiment for curries. Chutneys are also a good gift item that can be made in the summer, bottled, and available during the holidays as a small gift either alone or accompanied with a packet of curry seasonings.

APRICOT, NECTARINE, OR PEACH CHUTNEY

1-1/4 cups apricot, peach or other fruit vinegar
1-3/4 cups sugar
1 vanilla bean, split open
2-1/2 pounds ripe apricots, nectarines, or peaches
2 oranges
1 lemon
3 medium white onions
6 sweet red peppers or pimento
1 cup seedless raisins
4 ounces candied ginger, chopped
1 clove garlic, minced
1 teaspoon salt
3/4 cup slivered almonds
1/2 cup apricot or peach vinegar or other fruit vinegar
1 teaspoon freshly ground ginger

In a heavy 4- to 5-quart pan, gently boil the vinegar, vanilla bean, and sugar for 5 minutes.

Wash, pit, and chop the unpeeled apricots, nectarines, or peaches. Add the fruit to the pan and simmer 10 minutes, uncovered.

Seed, but do not peel, oranges and lemon. Finely chop them and the onions and add to the pan. Seed and chop the peppers in larger pieces for color. Add to pan with raisins, candied ginger, garlic, and salt. Simmer 30 minutes, uncovered.

Add the almonds, remaining vinegar, and ground ginger to the pan and simmer, uncovered, another 30 minutes to reduce the liquid. Stir frequently to prevent sticking. Remove vanilla bean, and ladle immediately into sterile jars and seal.

Once opened, chutney should be refrigerated, but it will keep for several months. Makes 3 to 5 pints.

•

3
CREAMS, CUSTARDS, PUDDINGS & SOUFFLES

In recent years there has been a revival of homey, old-fashioned desserts. Creams, custards, and puddings, long relegated to cafeterias where they appeared as globby, lumpy, and otherwise unpleasant endings to a meal, have appeared in finer restaurants in a variety of fresh and elegant forms. Sometimes they have been used to excess, as in the requisite puddle of *Creme Anglaise* supporting the piece of chocolate decadence or whatever other dessert is featured. Regardless, puddings, creams, custards, and the like are very soothing, comforting, and delicious, and deserve to be revitalized.

Creme Anglaise, known in Italy as *Zuppa Inglesa,* and in English as pouring custard or custard sauce, is the first of a series of classics in this chapter. It is good served over cakes or fresh oranges or pears, and is often the base of desserts such as rice pudding. You can change its character by adding rum or other liqueurs, depending upon how it is to be served.

No matter how careful you are when making custard sauces on the stove, they occasionally curdle. If this happens, let the mixture cool for about 15 minutes, then whirl through a blender, strain and use. It will be a little thinner, but not detrimentally so.

•

The vanillin in vanilla beans is responsible for only about 30% of the flavor. There are more than 150 other organic chemicals that comprise the marvellous flavor of the vanilla bean. Without the vanillin, however, the taste that we associate with vanilla would not be present.

CREME ANGLAISE: VANILLA POURING CUSTARD

*2 cups milk or 1 cup milk and
    1 cup light cream
1 vanilla bean, split down the center
6 egg yolks
1/3 cup sugar
1 teaspoon pure vanilla extract*

In a heavy saucepan, place the milk and vanilla bean. Scald, then set aside.

Place egg yolks, sugar and salt in a bowl and whisk until light. Add the milk and vanilla bean, stir, then pour back into the saucepan.

Cook over moderate heat, stirring until it thickens, but *don't allow it to come to a boil*. It should coat the back of a spoon if it is ready. Strain the sauce, then scrape the seeds from the vanilla bean into the sauce. Stir in the vanilla extract. Cool, stirring occasionally, and chill, covered.

•

This can be served on its own as the pistachios thicken it as well as flavor it.

PISTACHIO CREME ANGLAISE

7 egg yolks
1/2 cup sugar
pinch salt
2 cups milk
1 vanilla bean, split and scraped
12 ounces unsalted pistachio nuts, shelled*
1/4 cup pistachio liqueur (or substitute vanilla cordial or Tuaca)

*If you are unable to find unsalted pistachios, buy the salted ones, and rinse well in a colander.

Combine egg yolks, sugar, and salt in a large bowl and beat until thick and pale lemon-colored, 1 to 2 minutes. Scald milk with vanilla bean. Remove vanilla bean and set aside.

Slowly beat 1 cup milk into yolk mixture. Return yolk mixture to milk in saucepan, whisking constantly. Add reserved vanilla bean. Cook over medium heat, stirring constantly, until custard thickens; do not boil. Pour into processor or blender.

Meanwhile, boil pistachios in enough water to cover until soft, about 3 to 5 minutes. Drain well. Peel off skins. Pat dry with paper towel. Add to custard. Pour in liqueur and mix until smooth. Refrigerate until ready to use. Press custard through fine sieve before serving.

•

The same is true with this sauce, the macaroons providing the thickening in this case.

FRANGIPANE CREAM

2 cups milk
1 vanilla bean, split but intact
5 tablespoons flour
3/4 cup sugar
pinch of salt
2 large whole eggs
2 large egg yolks
2 tablespoons butter
1 teaspoon pure vanilla extract
4 macaroons, crumbled

Heat milk with vanilla bean just until milk is hot. Combine flour, sugar and salt in a medium saucepan. Add whole eggs and egg yolks. Mix well. Gradually stir in hot milk.

Cook over moderately low heat until boiling point is reached, stirring vigorously with a whip. Cook 2 more minutes, without boiling, stirring constantly.

Remove saucepan from heat and remove vanilla bean. Add vanilla extract. Add butter and macaroon crumbs. Mix well.

Cool, stirring occasionally to prevent a skin from forming over the top of the cream. Makes 3 cups cream.

•

On the back of many cornstarch boxes is a recipe for *Blanc Mange*. A more insipid, bland, and uninspiring recipe would be difficult to find. But *Blanc Mange* is a classic vanilla dessert, and as such belongs in any discussion of vanilla. Fortunately, Bert Greene has tackled the problem of "bland" *Blanc Mange* and has produced a vanilla *Blanc Mange* that is worth every bite.

BERT GREENE'S VANILLA BLANC MANGE

3 egg yolks
1/3 cup granulated sugar
1/4 teaspoon vanilla or 1-inch piece
  of vanilla bean
1-1/2 tablespoons cornstarch
1/2 cup milk combined with 1/4 cup
  whipping cream, scalded
3 heaping tablespoons vanilla
  ice cream
1 tablespoon unflavored gelatin
1/4 cup white creme de cacao
3/4 cup whipping cream, whipped stiff
3 egg whites, beaten stiff

Beat the egg yolks with the sugar until light. Add the vanilla, if using extract. Whisk in the cornstarch; then add the hot milk mixture. Beat until smooth. Add the vanilla bean, if using the bean.

Cook in the top of a double boiler over hot water, stirring constantly, until thick. Remove vanilla bean. Cool slightly.

Add the vanilla ice cream and allow to melt without stirring. Refrigerate custard 1 hour.

Combine the gelatin and *creme de cacao* in a small bowl; place bowl in pan of hot water. Stir mixture until gelatin is dissolved.

•

Combine the cold custard with the gelatin mixture in a large bowl. Fold in the whipped cream; then fold in the egg whites. Pour into a serving bowl.

Refrigerate at least 6 hours or overnight.

This dessert is of a soft texture—unlike a mousse or a bavarian—and is quite delicious with a fruit sauce, such as pureed raspberries, or a delicate chocolate sauce. Serves 6 to 8.

•

Creme Brulee, with its hardened carmelized topping, is sensuously good. Peter Feibleman, in *Eating Together, Recollections and Recipes*, comments about two recipes of his which he feels are right for seducing a person with a meal. He suggests Oyster Pie and *Creme Brulee*. He says, however that to serve both at the same meal, "would be considered overshooting the field." You will need to read his charming book, co-authored with the late Lillian Hellman, for the recipe for Oyster Pie, but here is my version of *Creme Brulee*.

CREME BRULEE

1 quart whipping cream
1/4 cup sugar
1 tablespoon pure vanilla extract
pinch salt
8 egg yolks
dark brown sugar

Preheat oven to 350 degrees. Combine cream, sugar, vanilla and salt in a heavy saucepan and warm slowly over low heat until cream is scalded, stirring occasionally. Meanwhile, beat yolks, in stainless steel bowl until lemon-colored. Very slowly pour hot cream into yolks; do not beat or mixture will foam.

Pour into individual 6 ounce ramekins, 6 to 8 cup pie plate, or shallow 2 quart casserole. Place in larger baking pan. Fill pan with hot water so water comes halfway up custard container. Bake until knife inserted 1 inch from edge of custard comes out clean (center will be soft), about 25 to 30 minutes. Remove custard from water bath and allow to cool, then cover and refrigerate overnight.

Preheat broiler. Sift enough brown sugar for 1/4-inch even layer over top of custard. Place custard under broiler 6 to 8 inches from heat. Watch carefully as sugar will melt in 1 to 2 minutes; do not let burn. Turn the containers if necessary. When sugar is melted return immediately to refrigerator. Serve very cold. The sugar topping will hold for 4 to 6 hours. Serves 6 to 8.

Vanilla was very popular in 19th century England, enough so, that in 1845, Sydney Smith gave meaning to a compliment of his "Ah, you flavor everything: you are the vanilla of society."

Creme Patissiere is the rich custard-cream filling found in eclairs, some cakes, and fruit tarts or pies (as in Banana-Cream Pie) that calls for a rich, creamy filling.

CREME PATISSIERE

1-1/2 cups scalded milk
vanilla bean
1/2 cup sugar
4 egg yolks
1/4 cup flour
pure vanilla extract to taste
2 tablespoons butter
1/2 cup cream, whipped (optional)

Scald milk with vanilla bean. Mix in a saucepan 1/2 cup sugar and 4 egg yolks, mixing until creamy and light. Add 1/4 cup flour, mixing just enough to blend. Add the scalded milk gradually, stirring until well combined.

Cook over low heat, stirring with a whisk until the cream comes to the boiling point.

Remove from the heat, remove vanilla bean, and add more vanilla to taste. Strain through a sieve. Allow to cool, stirring occasionally. When completely cool add whipped cream if a lighter, richer pastry cream is desired.

●

This is another of my favorite desserts, simple, nourishing, and just plain good. I once took a bowl of this to my country neighbor children who were sick with the flu and at home alone. The boys looked at the bowl curiously then one spoke up and said, "Just what is this?" I replied, "It's fish-eye pudding, and very good for the flu." They were young enough to eat it with no further explanation, and it has remained fish-eye pudding in our household ever since.

TAPIOCA PUDDING

3 cups milk
1 vanilla bean, split down center
2 large eggs, separated
1/2 cup brown sugar or maple syrup
   (reduce milk by 1/3 cup if using
   maple syrup)
1/4 cup quick-cooking tapioca
1/3 cup heavy cream
2 teaspoons vanilla sugar

Heat 2-3/4 cups of the milk with the vanilla bean. Beat the egg yolks and add remaining 1/4 cup milk, 1/4 cup of the sugar and a pinch of salt. Mix well.

Add to hot milk along with the tapioca. Stir and cook over very low heat until the mixture has thickened and the tapioca is transparent, 10 to 15 minutes. Remove from heat and remove vanilla bean, scraping seeds into mixture.

Beat egg whites until they stand in soft stiff peaks, then beat in the remaining 1/4 cup of sugar. Fold into the pudding mixture. Cool.

Combine the cream and sugar and beat until cream stands in soft stiff peaks. Serve over pudding.

Fresh fruits such as bananas, raspberries, strawberries, peaches, or applesauce are nice additions to tapioca pudding.

When my daughter was small, I would make rice pudding for dessert and then serve it the next morning for breakfast. It became legendary among her young friends. Even if I was rushing and the cream curdled, this uncomplaining child would eat bowls of it. I still often serve it as a special breakfast dish, mainly because I love it so much but it seems a little extravagant to make it just for myself.

You can substitute 3 cups of cooked oatmeal for the rice if you choose or if you are trying to sell some stubborn soul on the virtues of oatmeal; it will help.

BEST ON THE PLANET RICE PUDDING

3 cups cooked white or brown rice
2 cups milk
2 eggs, beaten
1/2 cup maple syrup or honey
1 vanilla bean, split down center
1 teaspoon pure vanilla extract
nutmeg and cinnamon (optional)
1/2 to 1 cup whipping cream,
   whipped
walnuts, almonds, dried fruits,
   apples, chopped (optional)

Put milk, maple syrup, eggs, and vanilla bean in a heavy pan. Cook over medium heat, mixing with a whip. When the mixture has thickened somewhat, add the rice. When it is thick enough to coat the back of a spoon heavily, remove from heat, remove vanilla bean and scrape seeds into the mixture, and add vanilla extract, and cinnamon and nutmeg to taste, if desired.

Put the rice pudding in the refrigerator and let it cool. Whip the cream and set in refrigerator. When the rice pudding has chilled, fold in the whipped cream and serve either at room temperature or chilled.

If the rice pudding by chance curdles, don't be alarmed; it will still taste good. Folding in the whipped cream will help some, and I've discovered that most people never notice anyway.

Serve fruits and nuts on side if desired.

•

Bread pudding is another old fashioned dessert that not only is delicious but also is a tremendous help in using up leftovers. Stale bread, baguettes, cookies, cake, biscuits—any of these things works well in a bread and butter pudding.

This particular recipe is from Cafe Beaujolais in Mendocino. Proprietress, Margaret Fox, has created a very special and unusual restaurant which features mainly breakfast and luncheon fare with occasional dinners and excellent desserts.

About this recipe she says. "Our staff goes wild for this dessert. I mean, they would step on each other's toes to get this. I have to remind them to leave some for the customers—'you know, these nice people who make it possible for you to be here.'"

The only change I might make is to add a little more vanilla and/or perhaps use maple syrup instead of sugar. But this is the recipe as Margaret makes it, and I'm certain you will like it very much just as it is.

MARGARET FOX'S BREAD PUDDING

enough very thinly sliced bread (no more than 1/4 inch thick), cake, or brioche to line the bottom of 8 x 8-inch pan
1/2 cup chocolate chips (or 1/4 cup raisins soaked in 2 tablespoons rum or brandy for 1 hour or more)

2 tablespoons unsalted butter
3 eggs
2 egg yolks
1/2 cup brown sugar
pinch salt
1-1/4 cups milk
1-1/2 cups heavy cream
1-1/2 teaspoons pure vanilla extract
1/8 teaspoon nutmeg
1/8 teaspoon cinnamon
whipped cream (optional)

Preheat oven to 325 degrees.

If using chocolate chips, sprinkle them on the bottom of an unbuttered 8 x 8-inch pan. If using raisins, strain and sprinkle them on the bottom of an 8 x 8-inch pan.

Butter the bread (or whatever you are using) and place it on the layer of chips or raisins. Do not (repeat do *not*) crowd the bread. It should not be wedged in. You should be able to see between the bread pieces.

Mix together the eggs, egg yolks, sugar, salt, milk and heavy cream, vanilla, nutmeg, and cinnamon. Pour through a strainer into the pan.

Push floating bread slices down into egg mixture. Set pan into a 9 x 13 x 2-inch pan filled partially with hot water. To do this in the most simple manner, put the smaller pan in the larger one and place both in the oven. Bring the hot water over to the pans, thereby avoiding the otherwise inevitable "hot water on the toes" syndrome.

Bake for 55 minutes. Do *not* let the temperature go above 325 degrees, or the custard will separate.

Cool pudding at least 1 hour, and serve with whipped cream. If you have some fresh raspberries, you might break them out at this point, too.

•

This is a dense Italian pudding, sort of like a ricotta cheesecake without the crust.

RICOTTA CHEESE PUDDING

1/2 pound ricotta cheese
1/2 cup sugar
2 egg yolks
3 whole eggs
1 tablespoon pure vanilla extract
1/4 teaspoon each salt, cinnamon
    and nutmeg
grated rind of 1 small lemon

Preheat oven to 325 degrees.

Put cheese through a sieve and mix thoroughly with sugar. Blend into the mixture 2 egg yolks, 3 whole eggs, vanilla, cinnamon, nutmeg, and lemon.

Pour the pudding into a 1 quart buttered mold, lightly sprinkled with bread crumbs. Place the mold in a pan of water, and bake for about 1 hour.

Unmold and serve plain or with vanilla sauce. ●

Pots de Creme, whether vanilla or chocolate, are very French and very good.

VANILLA POTS DE CREME

2 cups cream
3 inch piece of vanilla bean
1/2 cup sugar
6 egg yolks
1 teaspoon pure vanilla extract
    (optional)

Preheat oven to 325 degrees.

Scald cream with piece of vanilla bean and sugar, then cool slightly. Beat egg yolks until they are light and lemon-colored. Add the cream, stirring constantly. Strain the mixture through a sieve into custard cups, earthenware pots, or a souffle dish.

Set the pots in a pan of water, cover the pan, and bake for about 15 minutes, or until a knife inserted comes out clean.

Decorate with crystallized violets or rose petals (page 112), and serve chilled.

●

This is like a very rich, dense chocolate mousse.

PETITS POTS DE CREME CARACAS

2 cups light cream
1 vanilla bean, split open down
    center
4 ounces semisweet chocolate
6 egg yolks
1/4 cup sugar
pinch of salt
2 tablespoons vanilla cordial or rum
vanilla chiffon cream

Preheat oven to 325 degrees.

Combine 1-3/4 cups of the cream and the vanilla bean in a saucepan. Heat, add chocolate, and stir until chocolate is melted and thoroughly blended with the cream. Beat egg yolks until light and lemon-colored. Gradually beat in sugar and salt. Add the remaining 1/4 cup cold cream and rum. Mix well.

●

Stir in the hot cream. Remove vanilla bean and scrape seeds into mixture. Pour the mixture into *ramekins* or *creme* pots. Arrange in a baking pan. Pour hot water into the pan about 1 inch deep. Cover the *ramekins* with foil.

Bake 20 to 25 minutes, or until a knife inserted in the center comes out clean.

Cool and chill. Serve with vanilla chiffon cream. Makes 6 servings.

●

Most cooks have a favorite recipe for chocolate mousse, assuming they like and/or serve chocolate. Some are very thick and dense; others more creamy. Mine is lighter and creamier than many. It can be served in wine glasses with a simple biscuit on the side, or it can be poured into a mold with ladyfingers (see page 73) or even chilled, then piped between Swiss Meringue shells (page 83).

CHOCOLATE MOUSSE

6 ounces semi-sweet chocolate
2 tablespoons heavy cream
2 tablespoons vanilla sugar
4 large or jumbo sized eggs
1 cup heavy cream
1 to 2 tablespoons pure vanilla
*   extract, depending upon taste*

Melt chocolate with cream and sugar in a medium-sized saucepan, using a heat diffuser or very low heat. Stir, when melted, then set aside. Separate the eggs. Whip the whites until they have formed stiff peaks but are not dry.

When chocolate mixture has cooled, beat in egg yolks, one at a time. Add vanilla extract.

In a separate bowl, whip cream until it forms peaks but is not overly thick. Add a large spoonful of whipped cream to chocolate mixture, blend, then carefully fold chocolate mixture into cream. Fold chocolate-cream mixture into egg whites, stirring as little as possible, until just blended. Spoon mixture into glasses or mold, or place bowl in refrigerator until chilled. Chill well before serving.

●

VANILLA MOUSSE

1-1/2 cups sugar
1 cup water
8 egg yolks
seeds from 1 vanilla bean
1 quart heavy cream
pure vanilla extract to taste

Boil sugar and water rapidly for 5 minutes. Cool. Beat egg yolks on top of a double boiler and whip into the syrup gradually. Scrape the seeds from the vanilla bean, and cook custard over very hot but not boiling water, stirring constantly, until it becomes creamy and thick. Rub custard through a sieve and stir over bowl of ice water until it cools.

Whip 1 quart heavy cream until it is stiff enough to hold a shape, add vanilla extract to taste, and fold the cream into the cooled custard.

This can be frozen and served half-frozen, or it can be spooned into cups and served chilled. Decorate with crystallized flowers, shaved chocolate, etc. Flavored liqueurs can be added for additional flavor, if desired. ●

Charlotte Creams and Russes were extremely popular during the Victorian and Edwardian periods when most food was very rich and people neither worried about calories nor cholesterol. They are similar to a mousse, but a little more flavorful and not quite as heavy.

CHARLOTTE CREAM

3/4 cup brandied fruits (such as
    apricots in brandy) or 3/4 cup
    mixed glaceed fruit
1/2 cup fruit liqueur
2 envelopes unsweetened gelatin
1/2 cup water
4 eggs
1/3 cup vanilla sugar
pinch salt
1 vanilla bean, split down center
1-1/2 cups milk
1-1/2 cups heavy cream, whipped

Soak the brandied fruits or glaceed fruits in liqueur until ready to use. Soften the gelatin in 1/2 cup water and set aside. Beat egg yolks in the top of a double boiler or in a 1-quart saucepan. Gradually beat in sugar. Add salt, vanilla bean, and milk.

Stir and cook over hot water or very low heat until the mixture coats a metal spoon. Remove from heat and strain the custard into a mixing bowl. Scrape the seeds from the vanilla bean into the custard.

Mix in the gelatin, stirring well, and add brandied or glaceed fruits. Chill in a pan of ice water until the custard begins to set. Fold in the whipped cream.

Pour into a mold or line a mold with lady-fingers which have been moistened slightly with the liqueur and pour cream into the mold. Chill until the Charlotte Cream is firm and ready to serve. Unmold and decorate with crystallized flowers.

The following recipe is also an old fashioned one, known in English as Floating Island. I remember looking through my mother's cookbooks, especially the *Fannie Farmer Cookbook,* and fantasizing about Floating Island; it sounded so exotic. Somehow *Oeufs a La Niege* sounds much more exotic, but then, they didn't use much French in Fannie Farmer, so I never had the opportunity to compare the two.

OEUFS A LA NEIGE

2 cups milk
1 vanilla bean, split
6 egg yolks
1-1/2 cups plus 3 tablespoons
    vanilla sugar
6 egg whites
6 tablespoons water

Bring milk and vanilla bean to boil in a large saucepan over medium-high heat. Whisk yolks and 3/4 cup sugar in large bowl until thickened, about 2 minutes. Skim foam from milk. Gradually whisk into yolks. Return mixture to saucepan and cook over medium-high heat, whisking constantly, until custard thickens and coats wooden spoon, about 8 minutes. Strain custard into bowl and let cool.

Beat egg whites in a large bowl until foamy. Add 3 tablespoons vanilla sugar and continue beating until stiff peaks form. Fill large saucepan 3/4 full of water and bring to very gentle simmer over low heat. Mound whites into large puffs. Transfer to simmering water and poach puffs, turning over with slotted spoon, until slightly resistant when pressed, about 1 to 2 minutes. Remove with slotted spoon; drain on towel.

Combine remaining 3/4 cup vanilla sugar with water in small saucepan. Place over high heat and bring to boil. Let boil, without stirring, until syrup is medium brown and carmelized. Set pan in ice water until syrup is cool. Remove and let stand at room temperature. Do not refrigerate.

To serve, spoon custard into shallow bowls, arrange puffs of meringue over the top, then drizzle with caramel.

•

Flan is another classic dessert, served in Spain and Latin America under that name, and in France as *Creme Caramel* or *Creme Renversee.* For some reason, when we were children we didn't much like it. My mother made Flan occasionally and my brother and I referred to it as "flop." As an adult, however, I have subsisted on it at times, especially in Mexico where I consistently ate it for breakfast. This always seemed odd to the waiters which pleased me as I'm sure it added to their stories about eccentric Americans.

VANILLA FLAN

1/2 cup granulated sugar
1-1/2 cups milk
1 cup whipping cream
1 vanilla bean, split
3 eggs
3 egg yolks
1/2 cup vanilla sugar
3 tablespoons Tuaca or vanilla cordial

Preheat oven to 350 degrees. Warm a 1-quart souffle dish or mold by warming in oven for a few minutes or by standing it in hot water.

Heat 1/2 cup sugar in a saucepan over high heat until the sugar starts to melt; cook, stirring constantly, until it turns a rich golden brown. Remove from heat.

Pour caramel into the warm souffle dish, turning dish until all of the bottom and sides of dish are coated. Set aside.

Heat milk, cream and vanilla bean in a medium saucepan until mixture is hot but not boiling. Remove from heat.

Beat eggs and egg yolks in a bowl. Beat in vanilla sugar until light lemon-colored and mixture forms a ribbon when beater is lifted. Stir in Tuaca or cordial. Remove vanilla bean, and scrape seeds into mixture. Gradually pour milk mixture into egg mixture, stirring constantly.

Pour custard into souffle dish. Place dish in a baking pan and fill pan with water to halfway up the side of souffle dish. Bake about 1 hour or until a knife inserted into center comes out fairly clean. Do not let water in pan boil; add cold water if necessary. Cool flan on a rack, then refrigerate at least 6 hours or overnight.

To invert, run a wet knife between the custard and the dish, then place a serving dish upside down over the custard and invert quickly.

•

While working on this book I found some information on souffle making that I thought was interesting enough to pass along to those of you who have not had much experience making souffles.

To make a "Top Hat" on a souffle, smooth the top of the souffle when you have first poured it into the dish. Using a knife with a rounded tip, the tip of a teaspoon, or the index finger, trace a circle 1/2 inch deep around the top of the souffle 1 inch from the ege. The crust will break at this point and form a taller center. The souffle will also rise evenly.

The French method of baking souffles requires a hot temperature and a short baking period. The souffle is very delicate but will collapse quickly. The American method is at a low temperature for a longer time. The souffle dish is placed in a pan of hot water. The souffle will be firmer and more stable in the center and will hold its shape until it is brought to the table and served.

Serve the souffle in its baking dish. Break the top with a fork, then spread apart with a fork and spoon, using a tearing motion. Each serving should include some of the center and some of the bottom, top and side crusts.

Armed with this information, you are now ready to try any or all of the following three souffles.

Preheat oven to 325 degrees.

Butter a souffle dish generously then lightly sprinkle sugar over dish bottom and sides. Set aside.

In a medium saucepan combine the flour and 1/4 cup of the milk and mix until the mixture is smooth. Beat in remaining milk and 6 tablespoons of the sugar. Stir and cook until the mixture is very thick. Remove saucepan from heat and beat mixture vigorously for 2 minutes. Beat in egg yolks one at a time. Beat in butter and vanilla extract. Transfer the mixture to a large mixing bowl. Set aside.

Add salt to egg whites and beat until they are foamy. Add cream of tartar and continue beating until egg whites stand in soft peaks when beater is raised. Add remaining 1 tablespoon sugar and beat until egg whites stand in sharp, stiff peaks. Stir 2 tablespoons of egg whites into souffle mixture. Carefully fold in remaining eggs whites.

Spoon mixture into the prepared souffle dish. Trace a circle around top of souffle. Place souffle dish in a pan of hot water. Bake for 1 to 1-1/2 hours, or until knife inserted into center of souffle comes out clean. Serve immediately with Vanilla Sauce, or with a chocolate or lemon sauce. Serves about 6.

•

HOT VANILLA SOUFFLE

3 tablespoons flour
3/4 cup milk
7 tablespoons vanilla sugar
4 large egg yolks
2 tablespoons butter
2-1/2 tablespoons pure vanilla extract
1/4 teaspoon salt
5 large egg whites
1/4 teaspoon cream of tartar

CHOCOLATE AND VANILLA RIBBON SOUFFLE

2 ounces semisweet chocolate
1/3 cup granulated vanilla sugar
2 tablespoons unbleached flour
pinch salt
1 cup cold milk
1 tablespoon unsalted butter
5 eggs plus 2 egg whites
2 tablespoons pure vanilla extract

Preheat oven to 325 degrees. Butter and sugar a souffle dish. Set aside. Melt chocolate over hot water or waffle. Set aside.

In a heavy saucepan, combine the vanilla sugar, flour, and pinch of salt. Slowly stir in the milk. Bring to a boil over medium heat, stirring constantly. Reduce until mixture simmers, then stir the custard base until it is the consistency of a thick white sauce. Remove from heat, add butter, and stir until it melts.

Separate the eggs. Add 1 large spoonful of the custard to the egg yolks and stir well; add the warmed yolks to the custard. Reserve 1/4 cup of the custard mix and set aside.

Add vanilla to the remaining custard. Stir the 1/4 cup of reserved custard into the chocolate.

Beat the egg whites with a pinch of salt (and cream of tartar if desired) until they are firm. Fold two-thirds of the whites into the vanilla mixture. Fold remaining third into the chocolate.

Put the vanilla custard into the souffle dish. Pour on the chocolate mixture and gently turn and fold it into the vanilla base so that it forms large swirls. Do not overwork.

Place souffle into pan with hot water and bake for 45 minutes. Sprinkle a large handful of vanilla sugar over the top and continue baking for another half hour or so, or until knife inserted into center comes out almost clean. Serve at once.

When added to the heavy incenses and perfumes of the Orient, vanilla makes the odor more delicate.

VANILLA AND ORANGE SOUFFLE

2 tablespoons butter
1-1/2 tablespoons flour
1/2 cup scalded milk
1-inch piece of vanilla bean, scalded in milk
5 egg yolks
6 egg whites
4 tablespoons sugar
1 tablespoon pure vanilla extract
1 tablespoon orange juice
1 tablespoon grated orange rind
lady fingers
orange flavored liqueur

Preheat oven to 350 degrees.

Melt butter then add flour and cook, stirring, until the roux starts to turn golden. Add scalded milk and piece of vanilla bean. Cook the sauce, stirring constantly until it thickens, and then continue cooking, stirring constantly for 5 minutes longer. Remove the vanilla bean.

Beat 5 egg yolks well with 3 tablespoons sugar, and combine into batter. Whip 6 egg whites until they are stiff, adding 1 tablespoon sugar during the last minutes of beating.

Divide batter in half. Flavor half with vanilla and the other with orange juice and rind. Divide the egg whites and fold them into the two batters.

Put the orange batter in the bottom of a buttered and sugared souffle dish. Cover with the orange liqueur soaked lady fingers (about 1 dozen or so, split in half). Cover the lady fingers with the vanilla batter and bake for 35 to 45 minutes. Serve at once.

●

4
ICE CREAMS

Remember the word association game where one person would say a word and the other players would say the first word that came to mind?

If "vanilla" were to be said, my immediate response would be "ice cream." Everyone I asked said "ice cream" too. I would venture that it would be the response of most of us.

Vanilla ice cream seems to endure the ravages of time and the endless selection of flavors listed on the boards over the ice cream containers. The joke about the child who studies the list of 29 flavors for five minutes and then opts for vanilla is not as far-fetched as it may seem. Vanilla is still the most popular ice cream on the market.

There are three recipes for vanilla ice cream in this chapter as well as some for chocolate and assorted other flavors. Very cold foods often require more concentrated flavoring than foods served at room temperature. They supposedly need more sweetening as well, which is my major objection to most commercial ice creams—the compensation is too great, so the ice cream is too sweet. If these recipes don't seem quite intense enough or are too sweet, adapt them to your taste. Ice cream recipes can often be slightly adjusted without negatively affecting the results.

I asked Maida Heatter if she would contribute her favorite vanilla recipe to this book. She graciously consented, offering her recipe for vanilla ice cream. About this recipe she says:

Rich, luxurious, extravagant, delicious, de luxe, smo-o-oth; the best! This fabulous ice cream will not freeze too hard to serve easily—it will remain creamy and heavenly and perfect—even after days in the freezer.

A pretty reasonable recommendation, if you ask me.

In the days when the word vanilla was still considered synonymous with delectible, every soda jerk knew that the call of "Vanilla!" was the code word to alert the workers to come check out the entrance of a pretty girl into the shop.

MAIDA HEATTER'S FANTASTIC VANILLA ICE CREAM

4 cups heavy cream
8 egg yolks (from eggs graded large, extra-large, or jumbo)
1 cup granulated sugar
2 teaspoons pure vanilla extract

Place 2 cups of the cream (reserve the remaining 2 cups) in the top of a large double boiler (8 cup capacity) over hot water on moderate heat. Let stand, uncovered, until a slightly wrinkled skin forms on the top of the cream.

Meanwhile, in the small bowl of an electric mixer, beat the yolks for a few minutes until they are pale and thick. On low speed gradually add the sugar. Then beat on high speed again for 2 or 3 minutes more.

When the cream is scalded, on low speed, very gradually, add about half of it to the beaten yolks and sugar mixture. Scrape the bowl well with a rubber spatula. Then add the yolk mixture to the remaining cream. Mix well, and place over hot water again, on moderate heat.

Cook, scraping the bottom and sides frequently with a rubber spatula, until the mixture thickens to a soft custard consistency. It will register 178 to 180 degrees on a candy thermometer. (When the mixture starts to thicken, scrape the bottom and sides constantly with the rubber spatula.)

Remove from the hot water, transfer to a larger bowl, stir occasionally until cool, mix in the vanilla and the reserved 2 cups of heavy cream. It is best to chill this mixture for an hour or more before freezing it.

Freeze in a churn, following the manufacturer's directions. Makes 2 quarts. Note: To double this recipe you will need an extra-large double boiler. It will probably be necessary to concoct one yourself, by placing a large, wide, round-bottomed mixing bowl over a saucepan of shallow hot water. The rim of the bowl should rest on the rim of the saucepan.

•

OLD FASHIONED FRENCH VANILLA ICE CREAM

6 egg yolks
2 cups milk
1 cup vanilla sugar
1/4 teaspoon salt
2 cups heavy cream
1 tablespoon pure vanilla extract
1 vanilla bean, split down middle

In top part of double boiler beat egg yolks and milk until well blended. Stir in sugar and salt, and a vanilla bean, seeds scraped into mixture. Cook, stirring constantly, over hot water until thick, and mixture coats a metal spoon.

Cool, then cover and refrigerate until chilled. Remove vanilla bean, stir in cream, and add vanilla extract.

Pour into ice cream maker, and prepare according to manufacturer's instructions. When frozen, pack down, and allow to ripen for about 2 hours before serving (if you can actually wait that long). Makes about 1-1/2 quarts.

•

This recipe comes from the *L.L. Bean Game and Fish Cookbook*, written by Angus Cameron. It is a delightful and unusual recipe, one that would be fun to make for guests or for children, especially during the holidays. It is made with the extra-strength vanilla carried by the L.L. Bean Company (see the directory for purchasing vanilla beans and extracts). If you are using regular strength vanilla, use twice the amount listed in this recipe.

BUSH ICE CREAM

1-1/2 teaspoon pure vanilla extract
6 tablespoons sugar
4 beaten eggs
4 cups heavy cream
small bowl of new fallen snow

Combine all ingredients.

Serve immediately or place in freezer until very cold. For an easy adaptation, substitute maple sugar for granulated sugar, and top with maple·syrup.

•

One of the things that I very much like about Bert Greene's recipes is that they are incredibly sensual, almost decadent. When I was looking for the best ice cream recipes around that would incorporate a reasonable amount of vanilla, I found this recipe for Italian Chocolate Ice Cream in Greene's book, *Kitchen Bouquets*.

Here is a recipe that Bert made for his sister upon her return from Rome, as she had fallen in love with the intensely flavored ice creams of Italy. He says that when he himself finally got to Italy and tried the ice creams that his sister loved so much, he still preferred this recipe he had created from his sister's memory.

SUPERB ITALIAN CHOCOLATE ICE CREAM

6 ounces unsweetened chocolate, broken into pieces
2 cans (14 ounces each) condensed milk
1 tablespoon pure vanilla extract
1/2 cup unsalted butter, cut into 8 pieces
6 egg yolks
4 ounces semisweet chocolate
1 cup strong black coffee
1-1/2 cups sugar
1 cup light cream
1/4 cup dark rum
1/4 cup white creme de cacao
4 cups whipping cream
2 ounces unsweetened chocolate, finely grated
1/2 teaspoon salt

Melt 6 ounces unsweetened chocolate in the top of a double boiler over hot water. Add the milk, stirring until smooth. Stir in the vanilla. Remove from heat. Add the butter, 1 piece at a time, stirring until all butter has been absorbed.

Beat the yolks in a medium bowl until light and lemony colored. Gradually stir in the chocolate mixture; stir until smooth and creamy.

Heat the semisweet chocolate, coffee, sugar, and light cream in the top of a double boiler over hot water, stirring constantly, until chocolate and sugar melt. Stir in the rum and *creme de cacao*. Cool to room temperature.

Combine the two chocolate mixtures, the whipping cream, the finely grated unsweetened chocolate, and the salt. Pour into the canister of an ice cream maker; freeze according to manufacturer's directions. Makes 3-1/2 to 4 quarts.

•

This is another knock-your-socks-off, rich chocolate ice cream.

CHOCOLATE GANACHE ICE CREAM

2-1/2 cups whipping cream
8 ounces semi-sweet chocolate,
*   coarsely chopped*
3 tablespoons vanilla sugar
1 vanilla bean, split
1/2 cup milk
1 egg yolk
2 teaspoons pure vanilla extract

Bring 1 cup cream to boil in a small, heavy saucepan. Remove from heat. Add chocolate; stir until smooth. Set aside.

Combine remaining cream, 2 tablespoons vanilla sugar, and vanilla bean in another heavy saucepan and bring to simmer.

Whisk remaining sugar, milk, egg yolk, and vanilla in bowl until frothy. Whisk in 2 tablespoons of simmering cream mixture. Whisk back into saucepan and simmer until thick enough to coat back of spoon, about 5 minutes. Add chocolate ganache and whisk until smooth.

Cool. Transfer to ice cream maker and freeze according to manufacturers' instructions. Serve immediately or freeze until ready to use. Makes about 1 quart.

●

Not everyone is impressed with vanilla beans, as Marc Jones discovered early on when he met with a German pastry chef working at the Hyatt in Los Angeles. The chef was unfamiliar with vanilla beans, so Marc made his infamous creme anglaise, usually the perfect foil for converting even the most skeptical and discerning of chefs.

The chef lifted the spoon to his mouth, tasted the creme, and gave a little nod. "Yes, it is very good, but I would never use them," he said. Puzzled, Marc asked why he felt that way. "Just look at it," gesticulated the chef, shaking his spoon at the millions of tiny seeds in the creme. "No one would ever eat something that looked like our kitchen was filled with flies!"

BUTTER PECAN ICE CREAM

1 cup plus 2 tablespoons light cream
1 cup salted pecans
1/4 cup butter
6 large eggs
11 tablespoons sugar
1 cup whipping cream
*1 whole vanilla bean, split down
    center*
1 teaspoon pure vanilla extract

In small heavy-bottomed saucepan, slowly bring light cream to boil. Place in refrigerator and let cool completely.

Lightly saute pecans in the 1/4 cup butter. Remove the pecans with a slotted spoon and set aside.

Cream egg yolks and 5-1/2 table-spoons sugar; set aside.

In 2-quart saucepan combine whipping cream, remaining sugar and vanilla bean and slowly bring to boil, stirring frequently. Remove bean; scrape vanilla pulp from inside hull. With fingers, rub off any cream or remaining vanilla seeds and mix into cream.

Add about 1/3 of cream mixture to yolks, whisking constantly. Pour this mixture into saucepan, whisking constantly, and bring to just under boiling point. Remove from heat and whisk in butter. Immediately place pan in cold water or over ice to stop cooking. Stir frequently until cool.

Beat in chilled light cream and vanilla. Place in ice cream maker and churn according to manufacturer's directions. After churning, stir in pecans.

•

Fresh Peach Ice Cream: Make recipe for Butter Pecan Ice Cream, but delete pecans. Add 4 very ripe peaches, peeled and finely chopped after adding in chilled light cream and vanilla, and then churn.

Fresh Blueberry Ice Cream: Make recipe for Butter Pecan Ice Cream, but delete pecans. Add 1 pint fresh blueberries just before churning, or stir in just after ice cream has been churned if you would prefer to have the ice cream not stained from the berries. Any other berry ice creams can be made in the same manner.

•

This recipe is so unusual that it intrigued me. I decided that it would be fun to include, as there are so many good ice cream recipes to experiment with.

FRIED ICE CREAM

Cream Puff Shells:

1 cup water
1/2 cup (1 stick) butter
1-1/2 cups unbleached flour
5 eggs, room temperature
*1-1/2 quarts firmly frozen quality
    vanilla ice cream*

Beer Batter:

2 cups unbleached flour
12 ounces flat beer
2 eggs, room temperature
oil for deep frying
*pure maple syrup with 1 teaspoon
    per cup vanilla added*

For shells: Preheat oven to 350 degrees. Lightly grease baking sheet. Bring water to boil in medium saucepan. Add butter and allow to melt. Add flour, stirring quickly until dough forms ball.

Transfer to mixing bowl. Using electric mixer at medium speed, add eggs 1 at a time, beating thoroughly after each addition. Spoon 1-1/2 to 2-inch mounds onto baking sheet.

Bake until golden brown, about 40 minutes. Cool completely.

Slice partway through each shell and fill with ice cream. Wrap each puff with foil and freeze until solid, at least 1 hour.

For batter: Combine flour, beer and eggs in medium bowl and mix well.

Heat oil to between 350 and 375 degrees. Dip frozen puffs in batter and deep fry until golden brown. Quickly drain on paper towels. Place each puff in individual serving dishes and pour syrup on top. Serve immediately.

•

The Marquis de Frangipani, an Italian perfume maker who lived in the 16th century, had a passion for the combination of vanilla and bitter almonds. He scented or flavored everything that he made—including gloves—with this combination of flavors. It is a pleasant combination. The Italian sweet syrup, oregata, is a mixture of vanilla and almonds. Note also, the recipe for Frangipane Cream.

This is a good recipe to make for kids in the summer. Substitute maple syrup or honey for the sugar in this recipe if you wish.

VANILLA-CHOCOLATE CHIP ICE CREAM BARS

1 package unflavored gelatin
1 tablespoon cold water
2 cups light cream
4 egg yolks, beaten
1/2 cup sugar
pinch salt
1 tablespoon pure vanilla extract
2 ounces semi-sweet chocolate, coarsely grated

Sprinkle gelatin over cold water; let stand 5 minutes to soften. In a small saucepan combine cream with egg yolks, sugar and salt; mix well. Cook over moderate heat, stirring constantly, for 5 minutes.

Remove from heat. Stir in softened gelatin and vanilla extract. Turn mixture into ice cube tray without cube divider; cool. Place in freezer until almost firm.

Remove from freezer and place in bowl, then beat until fluffy. Spoon into ice cream forms or into ice cube tray with cube divider. If using forms, insert sticks at once. If using ice cube tray, wait until mixture is partly frozen to insert sticks. Freeze until firm.

To unmold, separate cream from the sides of the molds with a hot knife. Lift out carefully. Makes 16 bars of 1/4 cup each.

•

5

CREPES, WAFFLES, MUFFINS & BREADS

When I first began doing research for this book, I wrote to Chat Nielsen, Jr., of Nielsen-Massey Vanilla Company. I asked if he used vanilla in any unusual or special ways. He wrote back suggesting that I add a few drops of vanilla to the egg-milk mixture for French Toast.

His suggestion was for a simple, everyday food, and yet I can honestly say that it never would have occurred to me. I had used vanilla in beverages, custards, candies, and in baking, but I had not yet begun to use it as an everyday flavoring.

Bert Greene comments that vanilla, "tones down the egginess of the golden yolk." This is indeed true. It also adds a little zip as the natural sweetness in the vanilla gives grains a bit of a boost.

The following recipes are just a smattering of the types of leavened and unleavened breads we have available to try. Experiment with your own recipes for pancakes, muffins, and rolls. The small amount of liquid in vanilla won't affect the recipe, nor will, of course, the scraped seeds from the vanilla bean.

●

Because the synthetic vanillin is both inexpensive and very strong, it is used in industrial perfumes which are used to mask the otherwise objectionable odors of cleaning products, plastics, rubber, and paper products. It has even been used by tire manufacturers to help reduce the overpowering smell of new tires.

VANILLA CREPES

1/2 cup sifted unbleached flour
1 teaspoon vanilla sugar
1/4 teaspoon salt (optional)
2 eggs
2/3 cup milk
1 tablespoon safflower oil
1 teaspoon pure vanilla extract

Sift flour with sugar and salt; set aside. In a small mixing bowl beat eggs thoroughly. Add milk, oil and vanilla; mix well. Add flour mixture; beat until smooth.

Lightly grease and heat a 5-inch skillet. Pour approximately 2 tablespoons crepe batter into skillet, quickly tilting pan to spread over bottom. When delicately brown, turn to brown on other side.

Makes about 12 crepes.

This is a good basic crepe recipe. It could also be used for savory crepes; delete the sugar, and fill with seafood or vegetables.

•

Lemon Butter, or Curd, is a traditional English condiment used like jam for toast and scones. It also makes an excellent filling for cakes, tarts, crepes, and cookies. It would be excellent as a topping with either of the waffle recipes included in this chapter. I like it with *Creme Fraiche* or whipped cream.

STRAWBERRY-LEMON FILLED CREPES

1 pint strawberries
1-3/4 cups vanilla sugar
5 teaspoons pure vanilla extract, divided
1/2 cup butter
3 eggs
3 egg yolks
1/2 cup lemon juice
1-1/2 teaspoons grated lemon peel
vanilla crepes

Wash, hull, and slice strawberries. Sprinkle with 1/4 cup of the sugar and 2 teaspoons of the vanilla extract; let stand 1 hour.

In the top portion of a double boiler melt butter. Stir in remaining 1-1/2 cups sugar. Beat eggs and egg yolks; add to butter mixture. Blend in lemon juice and peel.

Cook over boiling water, beating constantly with wire whisk, until mixture is thick and smooth. Cool.

Stir in remaining 3 teaspoons vanilla extract and strawberries. Spoon about 2 tablespoons filling in center of each vanilla crepe. Fold into cylinders and arrange on platter. Serve, topped with remaining sauce.

•

CHEESE FILLED DESSERT CREPES

8 ounces cream cheese, softened
5-1/2 tablespoons butter, softened
1/4 cup vanilla sugar
2 teaspoons pure vanilla extract
1 teaspoon grated lemon peel
vanilla crepes
apricot sauce (recipe follows)
1/4 cup toasted slivered almonds

Preheat oven to 350 degrees.

In a small mixing bowl combine cream cheese, 4 tablespoons of the butter, sugar, vanilla extract and lemon peel. Beat until light and fluffy.

Spread each crepe to within 1/2 inch of the edge with cheese mixture. Fold in opposite sides, almost to the center; then roll them up. Arrange the crepes side by side in a buttered, shallow baking dish. Dot with remaining butter.

Bake, uncovered, for about 10 minutes. Serve with apricot sauce and sprinkle with almonds.

•

APRICOT SAUCE

2/3 cup apricot jam
1/3 cup apricot liqueur, orange
 liqueur, or orange juice
2 tablespoons butter
1 tablespoon pure vanilla extract

In a small saucepan combine apricot jam, liqueur or juice, and butter. Heat until smooth and well blended, stirring constantly. Add pure vanilla extract. Serve hot over Cheese Filled Dessert Crepes.

•

Serve Parisian waffles hot or cold with vanilla sauce, apricot sauce, fruits and whipped vanilla cream, or put 2 sections together shortcake fashion, and fill with berries and whipped vanilla cream.

PARISIAN WAFFLES

1 cup vanilla sugar
2 teaspoons pure vanilla extract
1/2 cup (1 stick) softened butter
4 large eggs, separated
1-1/2 cups sifted unbleached flour
1/3 cup milk or light cream

Gradually blend the vanilla sugar and vanilla extract with the butter. Stir and beat the mixture until it is creamy and lemon-colored. Beat in the egg yolks, one at a time. Add the flour and milk or light cream alternately to the mixture. Beat the egg whites until they have soft peaks and carefully fold them into the batter.

Heat a waffle iron just until hot. Brush lightly with melted butter. Spoon the batter into the hot waffle iron. Bake 2 or 3 minutes or until iron indicates the waffles are done. Cut each waffle in 4 sections.

Serve Sponge Cake Waffles warm with fresh fruits or homemade jams and whipped vanilla cream, vanilla chiffon sauce, vanilla creme fraiche, or a light vanilla custard.

SPONGE CAKE WAFFLES

4 large eggs separated
1 cup vanilla sugar
1/4 cup cold water
1 tablespoon pure vanilla extract
2 teaspoons grated orange rind
1/2 teaspoon grated lemon rind
1/4 teaspoon salt
1 cup sifted unbleached flour

Beat the egg yolks until they are light and lemon-colored. Gradually beat in the sugar. Continue beating until the mixture is thick. Add the water, vanilla, and fruit rinds, and beat well. Add the salt to the egg whites and beat them until they form soft peaks. Pile them on the beaten egg-yolk mixture, and sift the flour over them, and carefully fold them into the mixture.

Set the heat control on the waffle iron to low and preheat it 5 minutes, or until the iron is hot. Brush the iron lightly with melted butter. Spoon batter into the waffle iron and bake 2 to 3 minutes, or until the steam subsides.

___

Veteran fisherman use vanilla extract to wipe their hands before lake and stream fishing as the vanilla masks the odor of their hands and bodies from the fish.

___

VANILLA-BUTTERMILK DOUGHNUTS

2 eggs
3 tablespoons butter
1 cup sugar
3/4 cup buttermilk
1 tablespoon pure vanilla extract
3-1/2 cups sifted, unbleached flour
2 teaspoons baking powder
1 teaspoon baking soda
1 teaspoon salt
vanilla sugar or vanilla confectioners
    sugar icing

In a large mixing bowl beat eggs well; blend in butter. Gradually add sugar, then buttermilk and vanilla extract, beating well. Sift flour with baking powder, baking soda, and salt. Add flour mixture all at once to sugar mixture. Blend just until smooth. Cover and refrigerate for 1 hour.

On floured board roll dough 1/2 inch thick. Cut doughnuts with floured 3-inch doughnut cutter. Fry in deep fat preheated to 360–370 degrees, until brown on both sides. Drain on paper toweling.

Shake a few warm doughnuts at a time in a paper bag containing vanilla sugar or spread cool doughnuts with vanilla confectioners icing. Makes about 2 dozen doughnuts.

•

These muffins have a very nice flavor, but do not taste alcoholic as only the flavor is left from the cordial. Good for a brunch.

VANILLA PECAN MUFFINS

1-1/2 cups unbleached flour
2 teaspoons baking powder
pinch of nutmeg and cinnamon
1-3/4 cups coarsely broken, toasted
    pecans
1/2 cup firmly packed dark brown
    sugar
1/2 cup butter, melted
1/3 cup milk
1/4 cup vanilla cordial
1 egg, room temperature
1 teaspoon pure vanilla extract

Preheat oven to 400 degrees.

Generously grease muffin cups or line with paper baking cups. Mix flour, baking powder, and spices in large bowl. Stir in pecans.

Whisk sugar, butter, milk, cordial, and egg and vanilla in medium bowl. Make well in center of dry ingredients. Add butter mixture to well; stir into dry ingredients until just blended (batter will be lumpy). Spoon batter into prepared cups, filling each 3/4 full.

Bake until muffins are brown, and tester inserted comes out clean, about 20 minutes. Cool for about 5 minutes before serving. Makes about 12.

•

This is a dessert muffin, easy to take on picnics, or put in a lunch bag, but equally delicious served warm with good ice cream.

FUDGE MUFFINS

5 ounces semisweet chocolate,
  coarsely chopped
2 ounces unsweetened chocolate,
  coarsely chopped
1/3 cup butter
3/4 cup sour cream
2/3 cup firmly packed brown sugar
1/4 cup light corn syrup
1 egg, room temperature
1 tablespoon pure vanilla extract
1-1/2 cups unbleached flour
1 teaspoon baking soda
1 cup chopped pecans or walnuts

Preheat oven to 400 degrees.

Line muffin tins with foil baking cups. Melt chocolates and butter in medium bowl set over saucepan of barely simmering water. Stir until smooth. Cool slightly.

Whisk sour cream, sugar, corn syrup, egg, and vanilla into chocolate. Mix flour, baking soda and salt in large bowl. Mix in 1 cup chopped nuts.

Make a well in center of dry ingredients. Add chocolate mixture to well; stir into dry ingredients until just blended (batter will be lumpy). Spoon batter into prepared cups, filling about 3/4 full.

Bake muffins until tester inserted in center comes out moist and almost clean, about 20 minutes. Cool 5 minutes. Turn out of pan. Serve warm plain, or split open and serve with ice cream. Makes about 16.

•

One of the pleasures of poppy-seed breads, sweet or savory, is the crunchiness of the seeds in an otherwise delicate bread. This is a nice recipe when you need to take something to a gathering but also want to leave something at home for later.

POPPY SEED BREAD

2-1/2 cups vanilla sugar
2-1/2 cups oil
2-1/2 cups light cream or
  evaporated milk
5 eggs
5 cups unbleached flour
4-1/2 teaspoons baking powder
1/4 teaspoon salt
1/2 cup poppy seeds
2 tablespoons pure vanilla extract

Preheat oven to 350 degrees

Generously grease 2 bread loaf pans. Combine sugar, oil, cream and eggs in a large bowl and mix on medium speed of electric mixer until well blended. Sift together flour, baking powder and salt. Blend into egg mixture on low speed. Add seeds and vanilla and beat until smooth.

Turn into pans and bake until golden and bread tests done, about 60 minutes. Makes two loaves.

•

Corn and vanilla are wonderful together. The vanilla seems to draw out the natural sweetness in the corn.

RICH CORN BREAD

1-1/2 cups yellow cornmeal
1/2 cup unbleached flour, sifted
1 teaspoon each salt and sugar

3 tablespoons baking powder
2 teaspoons pure vanilla extract
3 eggs
1 cup milk
1/4 cup heavy cream
1/3 cup melted butter

Preheat oven to 375 degrees

Grease a 12 x 16-inch baking pan or large cast iron skillet. Combine cornmeal, flour, salt, sugar, baking powder, and vanilla. Add eggs lightly beaten with milk and beat until the batter is thoroughly blended. Stir in heavy cream and butter.

Spread the batter into baking pan and bake for 20 minutes or until well browned.

•

SOUR CREAM COFFEE CAKE

3 cups unbleached flour
1-1/2 teaspoons baking powder
1-1/2 teaspoons baking soda
1/4 teaspoon salt
1-1/2 cups butter (3 sticks),
    room temperature
1-1/2 cups vanilla sugar
3 eggs
1-1/2 cups sour cream
4 tablespoons pure vanilla extract
3/4 cup brown sugar
3/4 cup chopped walnuts, lightly
    toasted
1-1/2 teaspoons cinnamon
1 tablespoon water
vanilla confectioners sugar
    (garnish)

Preheat oven to 325 degrees.

Butter a 10-inch tube pan or large square or oblong baking pan. Sift together flour, baking powder, baking soda, and salt; set aside.

Combine butter and sugar in large bowl and beat until fluffy. Add eggs 1 at a time, beating well after each addition. Blend in sour cream and 1 tablespoon vanilla. Gradually add sifted dry ingredients and beat well.

Combine brown sugar, walnuts and cinnamon in a small bowl. Turn 1/3 batter into prepared pan and sprinkle with 1/2 nut mixture. Repeat. Add remaining batter. Mix remaining vanilla with water and spoon over top.

Bake 60 to 70 minutes (less if baked in square or oblong pan).

Cool for 10 minutes before removing from pan (texture will be moist). Dust generously with vanilla confectioners sugar. Serves about 10.

•

When I was four years old, my mother taught me the nursery rhyme, "Hot Cross Buns." She then purchased some hot cross buns for us to eat, took them home, and served them warm with butter.

I was, of course, enchanted to be privy to yet another of the fascinating mysteries of life that grownups seemed to have in endless supply. And each year during Lent I would remind her to please get us hot cross buns.

As I was searching for unusual recipes using vanilla I came across a recipe for hot cross buns, and discovered to my delight, that the recipe contained vanilla. Although the buns are traditionally made in the spring and served mainly during Lent, they are really quite good at any time. I personally prefer them with currants and nuts rather than raisins, but I have written in the original recipe here. Prepare them either way. After the first day, split them open and toast with butter under the broiler.

HOT CROSS BUNS

2 packages yeast
1/2 cup warm water
1 cup warm milk
3/4 cup currants
1/2 cup each butter, sugar,
    and raisins
3 eggs
1 tablespoon pure vanilla extract
5 cups flour

Mix yeast with warm water. In a large bowl, mix milk, currants, butter, sugar, raisins, eggs, and vanilla. Add the yeast and flour, mixing well.

Knead the dough then place in a buttered warm bowl, sprinkle the dough with a little flour, cover it with a towel, and set in a warm place for 2 hours or until the dough has doubled in size.

Punch down the dough and allow to rise for another 30 minutes. Shape it into small round buns and place slightly apart on a buttered baking pan. Allow to rise till double in bulk.

Bake in a 350 degree oven until they are lightly browned and baked through (if not quite certain if they are done, tap lightly on the underside of one of the buns. If the sound is slightly hollow, they are done.)

Decorate with a cross of icing made with vanilla confectioner's sugar and a little cream, or simply sprinkle with vanilla sugar.

•

In the Russian bakeries in San Francisco, *Kulich* and *Pashka* are displayed for the Russian Orthodox Easter which usually falls just after the traditional Easter celebrations.

KULICH
(Russian Easter Bread)

2 cups milk, scalded and cooled
    to lukewarm
1 cup sugar
1 cup unbleached flour, sifted
1 package yeast dissolved in
    1/4 cup warm water
1 teaspoon salt
6 egg yolks
3 egg whites
1/2 cup sugar
1-1/2 cups sweet butter, melted
7 cups unbleached flour, sifted
1/4 pound each candied fruits,
    ground blanched toasted almonds,
    and raisins
1/2 teaspoon saffron in 2 tablespoons
    brandy
1 tablespoon pure vanilla extract
1 vanilla bean
12 cardamom seeds
confectioner's sugar glaze

Mix milk, sugar, flour, salt, and yeast into a large bowl. Set the batter in a warm place to rise for 1 hour, until it is very light.

Beat 6 egg yolks with a generous 1/2 cup sugar and incorporate the eggs into the spongy batter. Add, little by little, the flour and butter, alternately.

Combine candied fruits, almonds and raisins. Scrape the seeds from inside 1 vanilla bean, and pound 12 cardamom seeds into powder. Strain the brandy/saffron infusion and add the vanilla extract, vanilla seeds and cardamom powder to the liquid. Add to dough, and knead it until it is smooth and elastic. This may take up to 1 hour. Beat 3 egg whites until stiff and work into the mixture.

Line cylindrical Kulich pan, if using one, or grease bread pans or rounds. Put the dough into the Kulich pan or other containers and allow to rise.

Bake in a moderate oven (350 degrees) for about 1 hour.

Frost with a confectioner's glaze of vanilla confectioner's sugar and water. The bread is traditionally cut in horizontal slices from the top; the crusted and iced first slice is always saved to use as a lid for the cake.

For years the vanilla industry has prided in telling the story of the lowly Melipona bee, about the size of your smallest fingernail, who has been responsible for pollinating the wild vanilla orchids for centuries, but who went undiscovered by Europeans until 1836. Well, the latest research shows that the melipona bee may not be the responsible party after all. There are about 5 species of tiny hummingbirds in the area that have diligently pollinated the orchids, something everyone knew, though the credit went largely to the melipona. But there also have been ants climbing through the orchids, and they may well be the largest pollinators of the orchids. If this is true, a number of people in the vanilla industry are going to be chagrined. It's one thing to talk about a tiny bee gracing the orchid, but an ant?...

Kulich is traditionally served with *Pashka*, a very rich sweetened cheese, nut, and fruit dish which is molded and served at room temperature. Although the *Kulich* and *Pashka* are time consuming to prepare, they make a dramatic presentation.

PASHKA

1-1/2 pounds dry pot cheese (can be purchased in some specialty shops; use non-fat cottage cheese if not available, and strain out fluid by hanging in cheese cloth overnight)
1/2 pound sweet butter (unsalted)
3 ounces cream cheese
4 egg yolks
1-1/2 cups sugar
1 cup heavy cream
2/3 cup each chopped blanched almonds and mixed candied fruits and raisins
1 vanilla bean
Pashka mold or deep flowerpot with a whole in bottom for drainage

Put dry pot cheese through a fine sieve, then blend with butter and cream cheese to make a smooth mixture. Beat egg yolks and sugar and combine with cheese. Add cream and mix well. Add almonds, fruits, and scrape seeds from vanilla bean, then mix till fruits and nuts are well distributed.

Line *pashka* form or flowerpot with cheesecloth that has been wet in cold water and wrung out. Pour the mixture into the form and fold the cloth over top. Weight the cheese down well and allow it to drip for 24 hours.

Unmold the *pashka* and decorate as you wish.

●

This is a recipe for vanilla rusks, a toasted bread similar to zwieback, but with a little more flavor. Excellent for teething babies, it is also good with soup, or in tortes or Greek cakes that call for bread or cracker crumbs instead of flour.

VANILLA RUSKS

1 ounce fresh yeast
1/2 cup vanilla sugar
1-5/8 cup lukewarm milk
5 cups unbleached flour
1/2 teaspoon salt
5/8 cup butter, softened
1 tablespoon pure vanilla extract
1/4 teaspoon cinnamon (or more, depending upon taste)

In a large bowl mix 3/4 cup warm milk with yeast and 1 tablespoon vanilla sugar until yeast is dissolved. Add 1-1/2 cups flour and mix thoroughly. Place bowl in a warm, draft-free place, cover with a cloth, and let sit for about 20 minutes or until the yeast mixture is about double in size.

Grease two baking sheets and set aside.

Add remaining sugar and milk to the yeast mixture. Add the remaining flour, salt, butter, vanilla, and cinnamon, and beat the mixture until the ingredients are thoroughly combined.

Turn the dough onto a lightly floured surface and knead until it is smooth and elastic. Divide the dough into 4 pieces and shape each piece into a long sausage shape, about 1-1/2 inches in diameter.

Preheat the oven to 350 degrees.

Arrange the dough pieces on the baking sheets and put them in a warm place for 30 minutes, or until the dough has risen slightly.

Place the baking sheets in the oven and bake for 20 to 25 minutes, or until the bread is golden brown. Remove the baking sheets from the oven. Transfer the bread to a wire rack to cool completely.

Meanwhile, reduce the oven to 275 degrees.

Using a sharp knife, cut the bread into 1-inch pieces. Place the baking sheets in the oven and bake the bread slices for 2 hours or until they are dry and crisp. Remove the baking sheets from the oven. Transfer the rusks to a wire rack to cool completely.

Store the rusks in an airtight container. They should last for several weeks. Warm slightly with butter to freshen.

•

Mandlen is a German recipe, a common accompaniment to soup in many Middle European homes.

VANILLA MANDLEN
(Soup Nuts)

3 eggs
2 tablespoons vanilla flavored
   olive oil
1 teaspoon salt
2 cups unbleached white flour

Preheat oven to 375 degrees.

Beat eggs with oil and salt and stir the mixture into 2 cups flour to make a firm dough. Form the dough into pencil-thin rolls between the palms of the hands. Flatten rolls slightly on a lightly floured board, and cut into 1/2-inch pieces.

Bake on a baking sheet for 10 minutes, or until lightly browned, stirring occasionally so that they will brown evenly on all sides.

Use in soups as garnish.

●

In the import trade, vanilla beans are classified as a dried fruit because they are actually the edible fruit of the vanilla orchid.

However, if the beans are made into extract and then imported, they are considered perfume and slapped with an enormous foreign perfume tax.

6
COOKIES, TARTS, PIES & CAKES

Most of us have used vanilla beans or extract when baking cookies and cakes and making custards. As a child, the little brown bottle of extract was as necessary to my chocolate chip cookies as were the chips themselves. I was never interested in eating cookie dough, but I have vivid memories of adding the vanilla to the butter and sugar before it was called for in the recipe, and then eating as much of that mixture as I could. I must admit my fingers *still* lose control and head for the butter-sugar-vanilla mixture.

Selecting recipes for this section was difficult because most recipes for cookies and cakes call for pure vanilla extract, but not too many focus specifically on the vanilla flavor. I chose recipes that I felt were special or unusual or that were "very vanilla." We had fun sampling and adapting the recipes for a couple of months while I made my selections, but I'm relieved that it's now over as my clothes have gotten very snug in the waist.

●

This is an excellent version of the classic vanilla sugar cookie. I can't imagine any child (or adult) not liking this simple, delicious cookie.

Between 1 and 2 tablespoons of vanilla extract per gallon of paint help to mask the odor of the paint as well as to diffuse the fumes. Less vanilla is needed for latex paints than oil-based paints.

VANILLA SUGAR COOKIES

4 cups sifted unbleached flour
1 teaspoon baking soda
1 teaspoon salt (optional)
1 cup unsalted butter
2 cups sugar
2 eggs, separated
1 tablespoon pure vanilla extract
1 cup buttermilk or sour cream
vanilla sugar

Preheat oven to 350 degrees.

Sift flour with baking soda and salt; set aside. In a large mixing bowl cream butter with sugar, egg yolks and vanilla extract until light and fluffy. Stir in flour mixture alternately with buttermilk, beginning and ending with flour. Blend well. In another bowl beat egg whites until stiff but not dry. Fold into cookie batter.

Drop by tablespoonful onto greased cookie sheets. Spread and shape cookie with back of spoon into a 2-inch circle, 1/2-inch high. Sprinkle generously with vanilla sugar.

Bake 12 to 15 minutes, or until golden around the edges. Immediately remove to rack; sprinkle again with vanilla sugar and cool completely.

Makes 3 to 4 dozen cookies.

•

These cookies are very chewy if taken from the oven slightly early; they are crisp if prepared according to the following time and then placed in an airtight container when cooled.

THE CHEWY OR CRISP CHOCOLATE COOKIE

1-1/4 cups butter, softened
1-3/4 cups sugar
2 eggs
2 tablespoons pure vanilla extract
2 cups unsifted flour
3/4 cup cocoa
1 teaspoon baking soda
1 cup finely chopped nuts
(optional)

Preheat oven to 350 degrees.

Cream butter and sugar in large mixing bowl. Add eggs and vanilla and blend well. Combine flour, cocoa, baking soda and blend into creamed mixture. Stir in nuts if desired.

Drop by spoonfuls onto ungreased cookie sheet. Bake for 8 to 9 minutes. Do not overbake. Cookies will be soft. They will puff during baking and flatten upon cooling. Cool on cookie sheet until set, about 1 minute. Then cool completely on wire rack. Makes about 4-1/2 dozen.

•

The next two recipes come originally from *The Brownie Experience,* by Lisa Tanner (10 Speed Press). Lisa has a number of recipes using vanilla wafers as a major ingredient. I must admit I was a bit skeptical at first, but I decided to try one of the recipes as it was made from vanilla cookies and called for more vanilla. I was very pleasantly surprised, and decided to include the recipe in this collection.

Then we tried the Caramel Coconut Pecan Brownies, and were so taken by them, that I decided to use them instead. If you like brownies, I recommend the book highly. Do use pure vanilla wafers. There is one brand on the market that uses pure vanilla extract. I have added more vanilla to this recipe than it called for. I also doubled the vanilla wafer crumbs to 4 cups and used 1-1/2 cans of condensed milk as I wanted thick brownies. I will give you her original recipe with the exception of the increase in pure vanilla extract, and you can make whichever version of the brownies you wish.

CARAMEL PECAN BROWNIES

2 cups vanilla wafer crumbs, packed
1 14-ounce can sweetened
  condensed milk
1 teaspoon pure vanilla extract
1 cup coarsely chopped pecans
1/2 cup butter
1/3 cup brown sugar, packed

Preheat oven to 350 degrees.

Butter a 9-inch square pan.

In a small bowl, blend together vanilla wafer crumbs and sweetened condensed milk. Work in vanilla and coconut. Spread batter evenly in pan. Sprinkle top with pecans; set aside.

In a small saucepan, bring butter and brown sugar to a boil, stirring. Simmer 1 minute, stirring constantly. Carefully pour hot caramel mixture over pecans, covering entire top.

Bake about 25 minutes or until caramel is bubbling all over top of brownie.

Cool completely. Cut into bars with a sharp knife. Makes 20 brownies.

•

The second recipe I chose because pumpkin (and squash, too) are greatly enhanced by vanilla. This is a nice recipe to make in the autumn.

PUMPKIN BROWNIES WITH VANILLA FROSTING

2 eggs beaten
1/2 cup butter, melted
1 cup brown sugar, packed
1/4 cup honey
1 cup pumpkin puree
2 cups flour
1 teaspoon cinnamon
1/2 teaspoon each salt, baking
  powder, and ginger
1/4 teaspoon each allspice and
  cloves
1 cup chopped pecans
1 tablespoon pure vanilla extract

Preheat oven to 350 degrees.

Butter a 13 x 9 x 2-inch pan.

Cream together eggs, butter, sugar, honey, and pumpkin.

In a separate bowl, stir together flour, cinnamon, salt, baking soda, ginger, cloves, and allspice. Slowly add dry ingredients to creamed mixture, stirring just to combine. Fold in chopped pecans. Pour batter into pan.

Bake about 25 minutes, or until toothpick inserted in center comes out clean. Cool completely in pan on wire rack. Spread with vanilla frosting, then let set to harden, chilling if necessary. Then cut into bars.

FROSTING:
1 3-oz. package cream cheese, softened, 1 teaspoon cream or milk, 1 tablespoon vanilla, 2-1/2 cups powdered sugar.

Cream together ingredients, gradually adding sugar. Add more milk or cream if necessary to bring to spreading consistency.

•

Because Ladyfingers are often used in molded desserts and as I had included some desserts that call for Ladyfingers, I decided to put in a recipe for these delicate little pieces of sponge cakes.

I *love* Ladyfingers either in desserts or just by themselves. Purchased from old fashioned bakeries, they are usually good, but last year I made a cherry dessert for a column I was writing, and as I had a photographer coming to take a picture of the desserts I was featuring, I opted to use packaged Ladyfingers to save time. They were dreadful tasting—flat in flavor and full of preservatives. Needless to say, homemade are the best.

LADYFINGERS

3 eggs, separated
1/2 cup plus 1 tablespoon vanilla
* sugar*
2 teaspoons pure vanilla extract
2/3 cup sifted cake flour
vanilla confectioners sugar for
* dusting cookies*

Preheat oven to 325 degrees.

Butter and flour two baking sheets.

Beat the egg yolks with 1/2 cup sugar. Add the vanilla and continue beating until light and fluffy.

Beat the egg whites until stiff but not dry. Beat in 1 tablespoon sugar; continue beating several minutes. Fold egg whites gently into egg yolks in three parts, alternating with thirds of the flour. (Do this carefully, as the batter must remain light.)

Spoon the batter into a pastry bag fitted with a medium-sized tube. Pipe batter onto baking sheets in even 3-inch lines about 1 inch apart. Sift confectioners sugar over tops.

Bake until the cake springs back when touched, about 20 minutes. Cool on a rack then turn out onto rack to cool thoroughly. Store in air-tight containers.

•

Almost every country has a version of these buttery nut cookies. And each country has its own special name for the cookie and some reason for declaring the cookie was originally their own. I like to call my version *Suspiros de Vainilla*, which translates to the exotic and deliciously mysterious "Vanilla Whispers."

SUSPIROS DE VAINILLA
(Vanilla Whispers)

1 cup butter
1/2 cup vanilla confectioners sugar
1 tablespoon pure vanilla extract
2-1/2 cups unbleached flour
1 cup blanched ground almonds

Cream butter and sugar. Stir in vanilla. Sift flour and add along with nuts to the butter mixture.

Chill dough at least one hour, or until it is firm enough to handle.

Heat oven to 350 degrees. Roll dough into balls the size of large walnuts, and place on a ungreased cookie sheet.

Bake for about 12 to 15 minutes. The bottoms should not brown much. Cool cookies in pan on rack. When still slightly warm, crowd together and sieve vanilla confectioners sugar over the tops. Allow to cool a little more, then repeat with the sugar.

•

This is a chocolate version of the wonderful butter cookies on which the suspiros are based. This cookie is a little crisper on the outside and softer inside, and has a drizzle of chocolate over the tops instead of confectioners sugar. The two cookies served together are attractive and different enough to be compatible.

SUSPIROS DE COCOA

1 cup unsalted butter (2 sticks)
2/3 cup vanilla confectioners sugar
(sifted after measuring)
1-3/4 cups sifted unbleached flour
1/2 teaspoon salt
6 tablespoons cocoa powder
pinch ground cinnamon
1 tablespoon pure vanilla extract
1 cup chopped walnuts or pecans,
lightly toasted
2 ounces semisweet chocolate

Preheat oven to 325 degrees.

Cream together the butter and sugar. Sift in flour, salt, cocoa, and cinnamon. Add the vanilla and nuts and stir well.

Shape dough into ball.

Shape into balls about the size of walnuts, and place on an ungreased cookie sheet, leaving about 1 inch between cookies.

Bake for 13 to 14 minutes, making certain the bottoms of cookies don't brown. The cookies will feel slightly soft when done. Cool on a rack.

Melt semisweet chocolate. When cookies are cool, drizzle the tops with a small amount of the chocolate.

Store in an airtight container.

•

The following recipe is for an aristocratic cookie. It is reasonably time consuming to prepare, but produces an exceptional sweet, one that will be extremely well received— assuming the recipients enjoy pistachios.

This cookie is supposedly best served the same day that it is made. Because it is time consuming, however, you may choose to make it a day or two ahead of time.

If so, there is a trick that I discovered a number of years ago when I wanted some freshly baked cookies for an impromptu dinner I had prepared for friends, but the only cookies I had were two days old. I put the cookies on a piece of foil in a moderately hot oven for about three minutes. After they cooled for another few minutes, they tasted freshly baked. My friends were impressed, and so was I. This only works for a few days after the cookies are made, but it's one way to get around baking just before guests arrive.

VANILLA CRESCENTS WITH PISTACHIO FILLING

3/4 cup vanilla sugar
8 ounces raw pistachio nuts, shelled
1 egg white
2 to 3 drops pure vanilla extract
1/2 cup unsalted butter, chilled
1-1/4 cups sifted unbleached flour
1/3 cup sour cream
1 egg yolk

Glaze:

1 egg yolk
1 teaspoon water

For Filling:

Blanch pistachios in rapidly boiling water 10 seconds. Remove and drain on paper towels. Wrap in plastic and refrigerate several hours.

Peel skins from pistachios. Put pistachios with 2 tablespoons vanilla sugar, 1 egg white, and pure vanilla extract, into a blender or food processor. (If neither is available, mash pistachios with a mortar and pestle, then add to other ingredients.)

Blend or pulse until ingredients become a paste.

Scrape into a bowl and refrigerate until ready to use (filling can be refrigerated for up to 3 days).

For Dough:

Cut butter into flour. Add sour cream and egg yolk and mix until smooth. Turn out onto plastic wrap and flatten into a disk. Wrap and refrigerate (this can be prepared 2 to 3 days ahead).

To assemble:

Preheat oven to 375 degrees.

Line cookie sheets with foil, and lightly butter foil. Divide dough in half, keeping one half in refrigerator until ready to be used. Sprinkle 1 tablespoon vanilla sugar onto a pastry cloth. Set dough on top of sugar. Sprinkle 1 tablespoon sugar dough. Roll dough out into a 12-inch circle about 1/8-inch thick.

Sprinkle top and bottom of dough with 2 more tablespoons vanilla sugar while rolling. Cut dough into 12 triangles. Shape half of the pistachio filling into 12 ovals. Set 1 oval at base of each triangle. Roll the triangles up from the base to point to form a cylinder.

Arrange on the foil covered pan. Shape into horseshoes. Repeat with remaining dough.

Bake 15 minutes, turning oven down slightly if necessary.

Glaze:

Combine 1 tablespoon vanilla sugar, yolk, and water in a bowl and whisk to blend. Brush glaze lightly over hot crescents. Continue baking until lightly browned, about 5 minutes. Slide foil onto rack and cool slightly. Then set crescents on rack and cool. Package in a tight container.

Marshall Neale said that his favorite story about vanilla involved a New York magazine writer who went to the annual convention of the Institute of Food Technologists a few years ago. She was taken aback by the proliferation of artificial, synthetic, and chemical additives that were being touted to manufacturers for use in food products. When she finally came to the vanilla booth, with their promotion of the pure extracts, she was overwhelmed. She said the vanilla was, "standing for all this world like a vestal virgin in a massage parlor."

These crisp little cookies are from a traditional Polish recipe. They are best served just after they have been fried. A nice afternoon treat.

VANILLA CRISPS

4 egg yolks
2 tablespoons vanilla sugar
1/4 cup clarified butter (regular
    butter will do, but isn't quite
    as good)
3-1/2 cups flour sifted with
1/4 teaspoon baking soda
1/2 cup sour cream
1 teaspoon pure vanilla extract
vegetable oil for deep frying
2 tablespoons vanilla sugar

In a large mixing-bowl, combine the egg yolks, vanilla sugar, butter, flour-baking soda mixture, and sour cream. Using a wooden spoon, stir the ingredients until thoroughly combined. Knead the mixture lightly, using hands.

Roll out the dough on a lightly floured surface until it is about 1/4-inch thick. Cut the dough into strips 1/2-inch wide by 4-inches long. Make a 1/2-inch slit near one end of one strip and pass the other end of the strip through the slit to form a knot shape. Continue until all the strips are used.

Fill a deep frying pan one-third full of vegetable oil. Set the pan over moderately high heat and heat the oil until the temperature registers 360 degrees on a candy thermometer.

Fry the dough pieces in the oil, a few at a time, for 3 minutes or until they are golden brown.

Remove the cookies from the oil using a slotted spoon, and drain on paper towels. Keep fried cookies warm while preparing the rest.

Pile on a warm serving plate and sprinkle the remaining 2 tablespoons vanilla sugar. Serve immediately.

•

When I was growing up I had an Aunt Oolie and Uncle Angus McGugan who lived in Canada and were of Scottish descent. Aunt Oolie always sent tins of homemade shortbread during the holidays. I was impressed by how the shortbread seemed to get better as it aged. When I was about ten years old I was given the recipe and then was sworn to secrecy as each Scottish family had their own recipe for shortbread. It wasn't so much the ingredients that were special, as they are about the same for all shortbreads, but rather the preparation that was a bit different.

Several years back I had a shortbread that was different from my family recipe. It was served in rounds as opposed to bars and had a crispness that our recipe lacked. I later found out that the crispness was from cornstarch and that the rounds are called "Petticoat Tails." I feel a little like a heretic, but I really like the crispness of Petticoat Tails. It is even more delicious with the addition of vanilla extract. I will share this recipe with you as I won't be breaking family rules, and the recipe is almost as good as the one from Angus and Oolie.

VANILLA PETTICOAT TAILS SHORTBREAD

2 cups unbleached flour
2/3 cup cornstarch
1/2 cup sugar
1 cup butter, room temperature,
* cut in chunks*
1 tablespoon pure vanilla extract

Preheat oven to 275 degrees.

Combine flour, cornstarch, sugar, butter, and vanilla. Work with hands until fine crumbs form, then work into a ball.

Press mixture into 2 ungreased 9-inch fluted tart pans with removeable bottoms. Impress edge of the dough with the tines of a fork, then prick surface evenly. Sprinkle dough lightly with sugar. Bake until golden, about 50 minutes.

Remove from oven; score each top into 6 or 8 wedges with a knife. Let cool slightly. While still warm, slide a knife between each cookie and pan bottom to release; cool completely. Serve, or store airtight at room temperature. Break shortbread along scored lines to serve, or wrap each piece individually and store in container.

•

These little tarts are simple and delicious, but also an unusual sweet to serve for large parties. They will keep several days before serving or can be frozen, thawed to room temperature, then warmed briefly in the oven to freshen before serving.

PECAN TASSIES

Crust:

1 cup butter, softened
8 ounces cream cheese, softened
2-1/4 cups unbleached flour

Filling:

1 cup vanilla sugar
1 large egg, lightly beaten
1 vanilla bean
1-1/2 cup chopped pecans
1 cup chopped dates
1 tablespoon pure vanilla extract
vanilla confectioners sugar

Preheat oven to 350 degrees.

In a large bowl, combine the butter, cream cheese, and flour. Mix until well blended.

Divide the dough into 4 equal parts, then separate each part into 12 balls, all the same size. Place the balls into the sections of 4 ungreased, miniature muffin or tart pans. Using the thumb and forefinger, press each ball into its cup, working the dough evenly up the sides to the rim.

Cream the remaining 1/2 cup butter with the vanilla sugar. Split a vanilla bean, and scrape the seeds into the mixture (save the bean to place in sugar or liquor).

Add the remaining ingredients and mix well. Divide among the unbaked shells, filling each completely.

Bake until golden brown, about 30 to 40 minutes. Cool on racks before removing the tarts from their pans. When serving, sprinkle with confectioners sugar.

•

Sweet potato pie is a Southern standard, kind of like pecan pie. Vanilla enhances the flavor of sweet potatoes in the same way that it does pumpkin or squash. This recipe will make 2 medium or 1 large sweet potato pie. If the sweet potatoes are especially sweet, cut sugar slightly.

SWEET POTATO PIE

3 large sweet potatoes
1/2 cup unsalted butter
1-1/2 cups brown sugar
1 tablespoon cinnamon
2 eggs
2 tablespoons pure vanilla extract
2-3/4 cups light cream
dash salt
dash allspice
1/4 teaspoon nutmeg

Boil sweet potatoes until done (about 45 minutes). Peel and cut into chunks.

Preheat oven to 350 degrees.

Put sweet potatoes and other ingredients into a food processor or blender, and mix until smooth and creamy. Taste for sweetness, adding more sugar if necessary.

Pour into unbaked pie shells and bake about 45 minutes or until pie barely jiggles in the center. Serve warm with whipped cream or Vanilla Chiffon Cream.

●

As you have likely ascertained by now, I really like Bert Greene's vanilla recipes. This one is a classic as it calls for *1/4 cup of vanilla extract!* (This is a good place to use the homemade extract that is sitting on the dark shelf.)

VANILLA TREACLE TART

Pie crust for 1 single-crust pie,
  unbaked
1 egg
1/2 cup condensed milk
1/2 cup light corn syrup
1/4 cup pure vanilla extract
1/2 cup ground almonds
pinch of salt.

Preheat oven to 400 degrees.

Roll out pie crust as thin as possible. Line a 9-inch quiche pan; trim edges and flute. Line pastry with aluminum foil; weight with dried beans or rice. Bake 5 minutes.

Remove foil and rice; bake 5 minutes. Cool slightly.

Beat the egg in a mixing bowl. Whisk in the remaining ingredients. Pour into a pastry shell. Bake 15 minutes.

Reduce oven heat to 350 degrees; bake 20 minutes longer. Cool on a wire rack.

●

This dense, creamy dessert is my own rendition of a pie I fell in love with in the 1970's. I loved the creaminess of the pie offered in a local restaurant, but I wanted something other than a graham cracker crust, and I wanted as little sugar as possible. This is what emerged.

YOGHURT CHEESE PIE

Crust:

5 to 6 ounces of good shortbread
  or sugar cookies
3 tablespoons melted butter
1 tablespoon cinnamon (optional)

Filling:

11 to 12 ounces cream cheese,
 preferably the natural cream
 cheese without stabilizers
1 container or 8 ounces plain or
 vanilla yoghurt
1/2 cup brown sugar
3 large eggs
grated peel of one lemon
1 tablespoon pure vanilla extract

Topping:

3/4 cup thick yoghurt, kefir cheese,
 or sour cream
1 tablespoon pure vanilla extract
3 to 4 tablespoons sugar

Preheat oven to 350 degrees.

Run the cookies through a blender or food processor. Mix with melted butter, add cinnamon if desired, and pat into a 9-inch pie pan.

Run the filling ingredients through a blender or food processor until smooth, and pour into the crust.

Bake the pie for about 20 minutes, or until the pie is almost set when jiggled. (I get furious when I'm making something like this and it cooks too much, so I tend to check the pie about every six minutes or so to make certain that it is baking evenly.)

Mix topping ingredients, spread on pie, and return to oven for 3 to 5 minutes, or until it has just set. Cool pie on rack and then place in the refrigerator for several hours until it is thoroughly chilled.

Top with fresh fruits if desired.

•

Vanilla is one of the three most common flavors used in pharmaceuticals, vitamins, and medicines. Vanilla may be the only flavor added, or it may be used as a base flavor with cherry or orange used in an overlay. Sometimes pure vanilla extract is used, and sometimes the synthetic vanillin is used in the medicines and vitamins. Banana, pineapple, coconut or bubble gum flavors are also sometimes used in medicines as they are all compatible with the flavor of vanilla.

When I was testing recipes for this book I tried a recipe for Butterscotch Sauce that sounded wonderful. It *was* wonderful—but not on ice cream. It had too much butter which clumped on the ice cream and didn't impart the smooth texture that sauces should have. I didn't want to waste the sauce, however, because it was very silky when warm, and quite good.

I finally decided that it might make a nice cake frosting, especially on a carrot cake. I made my basic carrot cake recipe, warmed the sauce, then let it cool, beating it every 10 minutes or so until it was cold, and the sauce thickened quite nicely. I have reduced the cream and made a few other adjustments as it never got quite as thick as it should for frosting. But the combination of the cake and frosting is excellent. It would also be good on other simple cakes.

CARROT CAKE
With Vanilla Caramel Frosting

4 eggs
1-1/2 cups oil
2 cups vanilla sugar or brown sugar
2 cups unbleached flour
2 teaspoons baking powder
1 teaspoon soda
1 teaspoon cinnamon
1/2 teaspoon each, cloves and
    nutmeg
1 tablespoon pure vanilla extract
2 cups shredded carrots
1 cup nuts, coarsely chopped

Preheat oven 350 degrees.

In a medium sized bowl, mix flour, baking powder, soda, spices, and nuts.

In another bowl blend oil, sugar, and eggs, and beat until creamy and smooth. Add vanilla and carrots. Mix in flour mixture and mix until thoroughly blended.

Generously grease a 9 x 13-inch baking pan, or 2 8- or 9-inch cake pans.

Pour carrot cake batter into pan and bake for 45 minutes if using a rectangular pan or 25 minutes if using round pans, or until a wooden stick inserted in center comes out clean.

Cool pans on racks for 10 minutes, then turn out cakes onto racks if using round pans. Let cool completely before frosting.

Frosting:

1 stick unsalted butter
1 cup (packed) brown sugar
1/3 cup light corn syrup
1 cup heavy cream
1 tablespoon pure vanilla extract

In a heavy medium saucepan, melt the butter and brown sugar over moderate heat. Stir in the corn syrup. Whisk in the cream, increase the heat, and bring just to a boil. Reduce the heat and simmer, stirring occasionally, until slightly thickened, 15 to 20 minutes.

Remove from the heat, stir in the vanilla, and place in refrigerator to cool. When mixture is cool beat with wire whisk until frosting thickens. Spread on cakes.

●

Everyone has a favorite chocolate cake recipe. And each one is the best cake ever! I decided to include the recipe *I* most often make for picnics or group gatherings.

I have a real passion for raspberry jam between the layers of cake, with or without the frosting between the layers. I'm sure that this is partly because I had an aunt Patricia, for whom I was named, who came to stay with us for a while when I was five years old. She was young, pretty, and talented, and I liked being with her. She made chocolate cake with thick strawberry jam spread between the layers of cake and a rich chocolate icing over the top. If you don't share this passion, stay with the icing only. The frosting that we use for this cake is *very* good. It is as rich and delicate as the centers of truffles.

SOUR CREAM CHOCOLATE CAKE

Mix together:

1-1/2 cups thick sour cream
1-1/2 cups vanilla sugar
4 teaspoons pure vanilla extract
2 tablespoons butter, melted

Sift together and add:

scant 2-1/4 cups unbleached flour
1/2 cup unsweetened cocoa
1-1/2 teaspoons baking soda
1/2 teaspoon salt
1 cup coarsely chopped nuts
(optional)

Beat in one at a time:

4 eggs

Preheat oven to 350 degrees.

Bake in 2 8- or 9-inch round cake pans or one 9 x 13 x 2-inch pan, well greased, for about 20 minutes or until top springs back when touched.

Cool on rack for 10 minutes. Remove the cake from the round pans and finish cooling on rack. When completely cool, frost with truffle frosting.

If you wish, split each of the layers in half and fill with jam or jam and frosting. Cover top and sides with frosting.

•

TRUFFLE FROSTING

1 cup vanilla sugar
1 cup heavy cream
4 ounces unsweetened chocolate
1/4 pound unsalted butter
pinch salt
1 tablespoon pure vanilla extract
nuts to decorate (optional)

Place sugar and cream in a heavy, medium-sized saucepan, and bring mixture to a boil. Reduce to a simmer and cook for 8 minutes. Remove from heat and add chocolate and butter cut into little pieces. Mix well.

When chocolate and butter have melted, add pinch of salt and vanilla extract. Place in refrigerator until mixture has cooled. Beat with a whisk until mixture becomes thick enough to frost cake.

At one time the word "vanilla" was synonymous with the best, having as William Safire said, "...the essence of zest and flavor."

Alas, like so many things in our consumer-happy world, vanilla has taken a real beating. With ice cream flavors as exotic as Double Mocha Almond Chip or Very Berry Bubble Gum, vanilla has become insipid, dull, and ordinary, in the minds of a great many people. Now it is considered "plain vanilla."

This has even carried over into areas other than food. An article in Business Week stated that, "Learjet now builds a standard 'vanilla' airplane—free of paint, upholstery, or any optional avionics or conveniences." Time magazine makes reference to "What the trade calls a 'plain vanilla' radio i.e., one without options." Even Newsweek reported on a dull movie: "After it's over you feel a vanilla chill settling over history itself."

One possible consolation is that over time people tend to tire of the new and faddish, and often return to simpler things. My guess is that with the increasing use of vanilla beans and quality extracts in our cooking, that people will respond to this "new flavor." Then vanilla will again emerge as the quintessential flavoring, at the top where it belongs.

This is a wonderful poundcake. It is moist, rich, delicate and not too sweet and it absolutely exudes vanilla. It keeps well. If it becomes a little dry before you finish it, serve *Creme Anglaise* on the side, or use the cake in Bread Pudding. It's good by itself, but with the addition of fruits and / or nuts and a syrup flavored with vanilla and / or liqueurs, it becomes an elegant holiday gift.

VANILLA POUNDCAKE

1 high-quality vanilla bean, split or cut into pieces
1 cup milk, room temperature
4 cups flour, sifted
1 tablespoon baking powder
1/2 teaspoon salt
2 cups unsalted butter, softened to room temperature
2-1/2 cups vanilla sugar
6 jumbo eggs, room temperature
1 tablespoon pure vanilla extract
vanilla confectioners sugar

Preheat oven to 350 degrees.

Pour milk into a saucepan, add the vanilla bean, and scald the milk. Let mixture cool to room temperature. Remove vanilla bean and set aside.

Resift the flour with the baking powder and the salt onto a sheet of waxed paper; set aside.

In a large bowl, cream the butter with an electric mixer on moderately high speed until light; about 3 minutes.

Add the vanilla sugar in two portions, beating thoroughly after each portion is added. Beat in eggs, one at a time, periodically scraping down the sides of the bowl to ensure an even mixture. Blend in vanilla extract.

On low speed, add the sifted dry ingredients alternately with the milk, beginning and ending with the dry ingredients.

Pour and scrape the batter into a lightly buttered, floured 10-inch tube pan. Bake the cake on the lower level rack of the oven for about 1 hour, or until a toothpick inserted into the cake emerges clean and dry.

Cook cake in the pan on a rack for 10 minutes, then invert onto a second rack. Invert again to cool the cake right side up.

Dust top of cake with confectioners sugar before serving, if desired. Or, drizzle Syrup over the top (see recipe below).

SYRUP

vanilla bean pieces
1/4 cup sugar
1/4 cup light corn syrup
3/4 cup water

Combine the vanilla bean pieces saved from the poundcake in a 1-1/2 to 2 quart pan along with the sugar, corn syrup, and water. Stir over medium-high heat until the mixture simmers. Without stirring, continue to heat until mixture boils. Cover and let boil until sugar dissolves and liquid is clear, about 1 minute.

Remove from heat, uncover, and let stand 5 minutes. (If made ahead of time, warm just before adding to cake.)

Using a toothpick or skewer, poke holes all over the cake top. Then spoon in syrup slowly so that it's all absorbed into the cake.

●

Although the directions suggest making the meringue into two large shells, it can be made into small individual shells. I really prefer meringue to shortcake when fresh berries come into season. It is lighter and I like the crisp outer texture and the hollow insides that soak up the juices.

SWISS MERINGUE SHELLS

5 egg whites
pinch cream of tartar
1 cup vanilla sugar
1 teaspoon pure vanilla extract

Preheat oven to 250 degrees.

Beat egg whites with pinch of cream of tartar until they are stiff but not dry. (Set the bowl with egg whites in a bowl of warm water. The egg whites will reach maximum volume when beaten over warm water.) Add sugar, about 1 tablespoon at a time, beating constantly until the meringue is thick and very satiny. Fold in remaining sugar and 1 teaspoon vanilla.

Oil 2 baking sheets and line with baking parchment. Using a 9-inch cake pan as a guide, trace 1 circle on each baking sheet, and spread them evenly with meringue. Bake for about 1 hour. Turn off oven and let meringue remain for another hour in oven if possible.

Just before serving, place one meringue on serving plate. Spoon or pipe vanilla whipped cream, or chocolate mousse on top. Top with second meringue shell. Sieve vanilla confectioner's sugar over top of second meringue shell. Decorate with berries or shaved chocolate. If not using meringues immediately, place in an air-tight container.

•

THE CREATION OF VANILLA

In the days when the world was young and the gods still came to Earth and mingled with its inhabitants, there was a beautiful young goddess, Xanath, daughter of the goddess of fertility.
Xanath came to Earth to visit, and while here, fell in love with a handsome young Totonac warrior. As she was a goddess and he only a mortal, it was forbidden for them to marry, no matter how great their love for one another.

Xanath was heartbroken. For a long time she grieved, then finally, resigned to her fate, she determined a way to give her love forever to her Totonac warrior and to his people as well. She turned herself into the graceful vanilla plant. Her vines lovingly intertwined with the trees that made up the jungle canopy. The beautiful yellow-green orchid bloomed, then bore the vanilla fruit, nectar of the gods. Xanath gave of herself fully, bringing happiness and pleasure to the Totonacs.

To this day the Totonacs cherish the vanilla plant and its fruit. The fruits have brought them health, virility, and prosperity. In return, the Totonacs pay homage to the memory of the beautiful goddess. The yellow-green orchids, which bloom for only a day, are known as Xanath.

Ancient Totonac Tale
collected by Hank Kaestner

7
SAVOURIES

Soups, Salads, Vegetables, Meats, Fish, Poultry, Entrees, and Side Dishes

---

There is some discussion among those who understand the chemical makeup of addictions, that those people who are "chocoholics," or consider themselves somewhat addicted to chocolate, may actually have developed an addiction to vanilla. Although chocolate has some addictive properties, there is speculation that vanilla is far more addictive. It seems to me to be a moot point, however. Whether it is chocolate or vanilla to which I'm addicted, it's legal—and delicious.

When I began the research for this book I was curious if vanilla could be used in non-traditional ways, especially in savoury foods. I searched for recipes with no success, so I decided to experiment on my own to find out if, indeed, vanilla and savouries would work or not.

The test recipe was to be chicken with tarragon in a creamy wine sauce. I boned the chicken breasts and made stock with the bones, onions, and a vanilla bean. Almost immediately the kitchen was filled with the fragrance of the bean.

Despite the delicious odor, I chided myself continuously, certain that I was about to ruin an otherwise perfectly decent entree, that I had wasted money, would horrify my family when they tasted this dreadful creation, and so forth. I held my arm out full length and backed off as I added a few drops of extract to the finished sauce, as if the chicken itself would rise from the dish in disgust.

And then I tasted it. It was delicious.

Since then I have found out that vanilla is used in savoury dishes in various parts of the world. Not only is it used in some Latin dishes, but Bert Greene reports that the Danes roast geese with a basting of rhubarb and apple sauce fully flavored with vanilla. In Provence, *quenelles de brochet* of ground pike are flavored with orange peel and a hint of vanilla. In a very pricey restaurant in Los Angeles, one of the featured dishes is lobster in a vanilla sauce. A cook featured in *Bon Appetit* uses vanilla in vegetable dishes. Sylvanna La Rocca —owner and chef of Made To Order in Berkeley, California—bastes her roast lamb with a rosemary and vanilla marinade.

Why vanilla hasn't made bigger news in savoury foods is a mystery to me. Perhaps it is because it was a rare and very expensive flavoring unavailable to the masses, so that it was reserved for sweets which were only for special occasions. I really don't know. But now that I have made this discovery, I intend to continue to use it as a highlight to my daily cooking.

The following recipes were tried by myself or by friends who were willing to experiment. I recommend that you be adventurous and try some of them or forge out on your own, adding a little vanilla to your favorite recipes. I will pass on to you a few tips I found in my experimentation.

In most dishes, the vanilla bean is superior to the extract. The beans have a fuller bouquet of flavors than the extract and are also a bit more subtle. In almost all dishes you don't need much extract; start with a few drops and add more to taste if necessary. Egg dishes, meat dishes, seafoods, poultry and game, and most vegetables benefit from it. I put some vanilla extract in the spinach ricotta cheese filling for a lasagne. It tasted great until I added the tomato sauce to the dish. Vanilla and tomatoes clash, at least they did for me in that dish.

Unless you scrape out the seeds from the pod, you can use a vanilla bean in stocks three or four times and still get decent flavor from it. Using a vanilla-laced cognac or brandy in cooking would be a good substitute for extract and would add a subtle vanilla flavor.

What follows is just the tip of the iceberg in the culinary sense; there are so many dishes vanilla can highlight. *Bon Appetit!*

Fruit soups are more common in Europe than in the United States. They can be served as a light first course to a dinner or as a dessert. They are especially refreshing during the summer when the fruits are readily available and the weather is hot and muggy.

COLD APPLE SOUP

8 apples
2 cups apple juice
juice of 2 lemons
1 tablespoon sugar or to taste
1 cinnamon stick
1 teaspoon pure vanilla extract
2 cups orange juice
2 cups whipping cream
3 tablespoons Cointreau or
*   Triple Sec*

Peel, core, and quarter 6 apples. Combine with apple juice, lemon juice, sugar, cinnamon stick, and vanilla in large saucepan. Cover and cook over medium heat until apples are very soft, about 20 minutes. Let cool, then cover and refrigerate 24 hours.

Remove cinnamon stick. Add orange juice and whipping cream to apples and puree in batches in blender until smooth. Pour into chilled tureen. Shred remaining 2 apples (unpeeled) and stir into the soup along with the liqueur. Serve immediately.

•

RASPBERRY WHITE
WINE SOUP

1 quart ripe raspberries
1 cup dry white wine
1 2-inch piece of vanilla bean
1/2 tablespoon cornstarch mixed
   into paste with 1 tablespoon water
sugar to taste
salt and white pepper to taste
pure vanilla extract to taste
1/2 cup each orange juice and
   white wine

Cook raspberries and white wine with vanilla bean for 15 minutes, or until fruit is tender. Remove bean and strain fruit and juice through a fine sieve. Return soup to the heat and add cornstarch/water mixture.

Bring the soup to a boil, lower the heat, and simmer gently for 10 minutes, stirring frequently and skimming if needed.

Season with sugar, salt and pepper and vanilla to taste. Add orange juice and wine and chill well.

•

MIXED FRUIT SOUP

1/2 cup each of some or all of
   the following:
peaches
hulled strawberries
fresh rhubarb
oranges, peeled and seeded
fresh pineapple
raspberries

3/4 cup sugar
2 tablespoons unstrained
   lemon juice
1/2 teaspoon salt
2 cloves
1 2-inch piece of vanilla bean
creme fraiche or sour cream

Combine fruits, finely chopped, sugar, lemon juice, salt, cloves, and vanilla bean. Add 2 quarts water and bring the liquid to a boil.

Lower the heat and simmer gently for 15 minutes.

Remove the vanilla bean and cloves, rub through a fine sieve, or puree in a blender. Add vanilla extract if desired.

Chill thoroughly and serve with a dollop of creme fraiche or sour cream and toasted crackers.

•

Both this carrot soup and the chicken soup that follows would be nice with the vanilla mandlen (soup nuts).

CREAM OF CARROT SOUP

2 tablespoons butter
4 to 5 carrots, chopped
1 onion, chopped
1/2 cup rice
1 quart chicken stock, preferably
   homemade, plus
2 cups chicken stock
1 cup milk or light cream
1 tablespoon butter
salt and pepper to taste
1/2 vanilla bean, split lengthwise

Melt 2 tablespoons butter in a sauce pan, add carrots and onion and cook slowly for 15 minutes, stirring occasionally.

Add rice, all but 2 cups of stock, and vanilla bean, and cook slowly for about 45 minutes, or until the carrots are done. Remove bean. Strain the soup through a fine sieve or run through blender. Add last 2 cups chicken stock. Bring to boil and add 1 cup milk or cream and butter.

Grate fresh nutmeg on top if desired, or garnish with parsley sprig.

●

CREAM OF CHICKEN AND VANILLA SOUP

1/4 cup butter
1/2 cup flour
1-1/2 quarts chicken broth
1 onion, chopped
1 stalk celery, chopped
1 leek, chopped
2 springs parsley
1/2 vanilla bean (or more depending on strength of vanilla desired)
2 egg yolks
up to 2 cups cream
salt and pepper
finely chopped scallions
1 cup finely sliced cooked chicken

Melt butter in saucepan, stir in flour, and cook, stirring constantly, until it starts to turn golden. Add chicken broth and cook, stirring, until smooth.

Add vanilla pod, onion, celery and leeks, and simmer for 30 minutes. Skim the broth, remove the vanilla pod, and press soup through fine sieve or run in food processor or blender until smooth.

Mix egg yolks with 1 cup cream and a little of hot chicken base. Stir the mixture into chicken soup, and bring almost to a boil. Correct the seasoning with salt and white pepper, and add up to 1 cup more cream to give desired consistency.

●

Peter Stone's first solo trip as an importer took him to the island of Tahaa'a (about 150 miles west of Tahiti). He spent his time searching for and purchasing roughly 100 kilos of Tahitian vanilla beans. The morning he was to leave, he rose before sunrise, packed the beans in tin boxes (which, until recently, was the regulation container for international transport) and went to wait for one of the small boats that weave through the island each day, picking up locals and transporting them to work.

Dismayed by the weight of the beans and worried that the boat wouldn't arrive in time for him to catch his return flight to the U.S., Peter began to question why he had ever gotten into the import business in the first place.

When the boat finally arrived, several locals were already on board. As Peter sat down, a couple of the passengers had guitars and started to play. Others joined them, singing traditional Tahitian songs. Just then, the sun emerged from the ocean on the eastern horizon. They sang to the sun, heralding it on its daily journey across the South Pacific sky. As the boat slipped through the canals and lush tropical greenery dipped into the water's edge, the voices of the passengers celebrated all that was good and beautiful in their lives. Peter says this memory is forever etched in his mind as one of the most awesome experiences in his life. And yes, he is glad to be an importer.

In the process of experimenting with vanilla beans, Mary-Pat Tormey of the Dynamite Mousse Company suggested that I place a vanilla bean in some quality olive oil to use on salads. Being somewhat cautious by nature, I bought a pint-sized bottle of light flavored olive oil, split a bean, and dropped it in. I then allowed the oil to sit in a dark place for about 3 weeks.

I had planned a simple dinner party for some friends who are European and are very willing to try new foods. I decided this was my opportunity to see what salad with vanilla dressing would be like. I had made a seafood lasagne which was rich and complex in flavor so I wanted a simple salad. The results were far better than I had anticipated. In fact, the dressing was so good that it will remain a classic in my repertoire.

TOSSED GREEN SALAD WITH BERRY AND VANILLA VINAIGRETTE

Salad:

fresh greens (red leaf lettuce, escarole, radicchio, etc.)
red onion, thinly sliced
cucumber, thinly sliced
alfalfa or clover sprouts
rose petals or nasturtiums, thinly sliced (optional)

Wash greens and break into bite-sized pieces. Place in bowl and toss. Add onion and cucumber slices. Toss with vinaigrette dressing (see recipe below). Just before serving, garnish on top with flower petals.

Vinaigrette:

8 tablespoons vanilla flavored oil
3 to 4 tablespoons berry vinegar (I use homemade loganberry vinegar)

1 shallot, finely minced
salt and pepper to taste

Mix all in a bottle and chill. Toss with salads just before serving.

•

This is one of my favorite winter salads.

GREEN SALAD WITH FRUITS

red onion, sliced thinly and broken into rings
1 ripe avocado
grapefruit or orange sections, or sliced papaya
alfalfa sprouts
lettuce greens, washed and drained
1/2 cup almonds, thinly sliced, and lightly toasted in oven

Cut avocado and fruit into sections or slices. Save any fruit juices. Set aside.

Break up salad greens into bite-sized pieces and place in bowl with onions and sprouts. Place fruit slices on top. Add almonds and dressing just before tossing and serving.

Dressing:

2 tablespoons vanilla olive oil or other salad oil
1 tablespoon apple cider or other fruit vinegar
juice of 1/2 lemon
1 tablespoon brown sugar or honey
1 tablespoon soy sauce
2 to 3 tablespoons juice from fruits (or whatever amount you have)
1/2 teaspoon pure vanilla extract

Mix together in a bottle or jar. Add more oil or salt to taste. Shake well and pour over salad.

This is an Australian salad which makes use of some of the many tropical fruits that grow there. Kiwi fruit could be added to this salad too, and the salad could also be served in hollowed out pineapple shells.

PINEAPPLE AND CABBAGE SALAD

1 pineapple, peeled, cored
   and cubed
1 grapefruit, peeled and segmented
1 orange, peeled and segmented
1/2 white cabbage, finely shredded
1/2 cucumber, sliced unpeeled
1 sweet red pepper, seeded
   and sliced
1 cup diced cooked ham (turkey,
   chicken, or shrimp could be used)
grated rind of 1 orange
4 tablespoons olive oil
2 tablespoons wine vinegar
2 tablespoons mayonnaise
2 tablespoons heavy cream
1 to 2 teaspoons pure vanilla extract
   (to taste)
salt
sugar

In a large salad bowl combine the fruit, vegetables, and ham. In a small bowl, mix grated orange rind, oil, vinegar, mayonnaise, cream, salt, sugar, and vanilla to taste. Pour the dressing over the salad and mix thoroughly. Adjust seasonings. Chill thoroughly before serving.

•

Here is another of my experiments, one which we liked very much. The salad can be served tossed, but it makes a very attractive presentation to arrange the lettuce leaves on a large plate or on individual salad plates, and place the various ingredients attractively after first mixing the seafood with a little of the dressing. Drizzle more dressing over the entire salad.

SEAFOOD-PECAN SALAD WITH VANILLA MAYONNAISE

1-1/2 pounds crab, shrimp, firm-
   fleshed white fish, or lobster
   (or a mixture: I used shrimp and
   sea bass)
3 scallions, including greens, finely
   chopped
1/2 cup celery, thinly sliced
avocado slices, thin slices of very
   fresh mushroom, artichoke hearts,
   or cherry tomatoes (optional)
butter or boston lettuce
1/2 cup pecan halves, slivered and
   lightly toasted
vanilla mayonnaise dressing
   (see recipe below)

Mix seafood, scallions, and celery together with enough mayonnaise to bind lightly. Lay on bed of lettuce and garnish with additional ingredients or break up lettuce into bite-sized pieces, place ingredients in a bowl, and toss, adding pecan pieces at last.

•

VANILLA MAYONNAISE

1 egg
1/2 teaspoon Dijon-style mustard
1/2 teaspoon sugar
1 tablespoon lemon juice
1 tablespoon fruit vinegar
1 cup vanilla oil or 1 cup oil and
*   1 teaspoon pure vanilla extract*

Place egg, mustard, sugar, lemon juice, and vinegar in a blender or food processor. Slowly add oil, a few drops at first, then in a slow, steady stream while running blender or processor.

After oil is added, taste, adjust seasonings, add more vinegar or lemon juice if desired, and use. If the dressing becomes too thick, thin with a little oil and vinegar, using a whisk to blend.

•

I used vanilla cordial as a substitute for maple syrup in this recipe. The recipe for vanilla syrup could be used instead.

VANILLA BAKED ACORN SQUASH

3 large acorn squash, halved
*   lengthwise and seeded*
salt
1/4 cup butter, room temperature
1/3 to 1/2 cup vanilla cordial

Preheat oven to 325 degrees.

Sprinkle cut sides of squash with salt. Arrange cut sides down in baking dish. Bake until tender when easily pierced with a sharp knife, about 45 to 60 minutes.

Turn over and run fork over the cut sides of squash. Spread with butter. Drizzle with cordial, then return to oven and bake for 3 more minutes.

SPICED SWEET POTATOES

3 pounds sweet potatoes
1/2 cup brown sugar or maple syrup
3 tablespoons butter
1/2 teaspoon cinnamon
1/2 teaspoon nutmeg
1 teaspoon pure vanilla extract
1 cup milk
salt and pepper to taste
grated orange rind (optional)
sliced almonds (optional)

Bake sweet potatoes until soft. Scoop out centers and mash. Add balance of ingredients to potatoes, and bake in a hot oven for about 15 minutes.

Garnish with orange rind and sliced almonds before baking, if desired.

•

The small amount of vanilla with the beans brings up their flavor.

ALMOND-VANILLA GREEN BEANS

2 pounds green beans, trimmed
1/2 cup almonds, sliced or quartered
4 tablespoons, unsalted butter
1/2 teaspoon pure vanilla extract
salt and pepper to taste
fresh lime juice (optional)

Steam beans for about 5 minutes or until crisp-tender. Drain well.

Saute almonds in butter until well coated and crisp. Pour over beans. Add vanilla, salt and pepper to taste, and a squeeze of lime juice if desired. Serves 6.

•

If you would prefer to have the cauliflower perfumed with vanilla, place a bean with the water when the cauliflower steams, and omit the extract from the recipe—or use both.

STEAMED CAULIFLOWER WITH VANILLA SAUCE

3 tablespoons butter
3 tablespoons unbleached flour
2 cups chicken stock
2 egg yolks
1/2 cup whipping cream
2 tablespoons minced fresh parsley
1 tablespoon pure vanilla extract
1 teaspoon fresh lemon juice
salt and pepper to taste
1 2-pound head cauliflower,
    with base trimmed off

Melt butter in heavy saucepan over low heat. Add flour and stir 3 minutes. Whisk in stock. Increase heat and boil until thickened, stirring constantly. Whisk yolks and cream in bowl. Slowly whisk in stock mixture.

Return to saucepan and boil 1 minute, stirring constantly. Mix in parsley, vanilla, lemon juice, salt, and pepper.

While preparing sauce, steam cauliflower until crisp-tender, about 25 to 30 minutes. Arrange on hot serving dish. Cover with some of sauce and serve, passing remaining sauce separately.

•

HONEY AND VANILLA GLAZED VEGETABLES

1/4 cup honey
1/4 cup butter
1 teaspoon pure vanilla extract
salt and pepper to taste

Melt butter in a saucepan. Add honey and stir until mixture is blended. Add vanilla and vegetables.

Cook slowly, turning occasionally, until well glazed. Serve.

The best vegetables to serve glazed are carrots, onions, beets and yams.

•

ORANGE AND VANILLA BEETS

18 small beets, cooked, peeled
    and sliced
3 tablespoons butter
1 tablespoon cornstarch
1/4 cup lemon juice
1/4 cup brown sugar
2 cups orange juice
1 teaspoon pure vanilla extract

Put all ingredients except beets and vanilla in a saucepan and cook until the sauce is slightly thickened, stirring constantly. Season with salt and pepper, add vanilla, and pour over the sliced hot beets.

•

Using just the vanilla olive oil will impart a delicate fragrance to this dish. Adding the extract will bring out the flavor both of the vanilla and of the zucchini.

ZUCCHINI FIORENTINA

6 baby zucchini, thinly sliced
2 eggs beaten
1 teaspoon pure vanilla extract
    (optional)
1/2 cup flour
1/2 cup vanilla olive oil
salt
freshly ground black pepper

Dip the zucchini slices in beaten eggs to which vanilla has been added, then in flour lightly seasoned with salt and pepper. Saute in vanilla olive oil about five minutes or until golden. Serve immediately. Serves 4 to 6.

•

This side dish is an excellent accompaniment for curries or stews. It is light, fluffy, and rather dry in texture, good for absorbing sauces.

RICE WITH COCONUT, VANILLA, DATES AND LEMON

1 fresh coconut
1-3/4 cups basmati rice
1/2 teaspoon salt
1/2 vanilla bean, split in half,
    lengthwise
3/4 cup pitted dates, thinly sliced
1-1/2 teaspoons grated lemon zest
1/4 teaspoon fennel seeds, crushed
3 tablespoons fresh lemon juice

Preheat oven to 325 degrees.

Using a screwdriver and hammer, puncture two of the coconut "eyes." Strain and reserve the liquid. Set the coconut on a shelf in the oven and bake for 15 minutes. Crack the shell near center with a few hard taps with a hammer. Pry out the coconut meat in chunks.

Slice the pieces of coconut into thin slivers until you have 1 cup. Save the balance of the coconut for another use. Add water to the reserved coconut liquid to equal 2-2/3 cups.

In a heavy 2-quart saucepan, combine rice with the coconut liquid and vanilla bean and bring to full boil over high heat. Add salt. Reduce the heat to very low, cover, and cook for 15 minutes. Remove from the heat and let stand, covered for 10 minutes. Remove vanilla bean.

Fluff the rice into a hot serving dish. Toss with dates, coconut, lemon zest fennel seeds and lemon juice to taste. Serve.

•

In Bert Greene's *Kitchen Bouquets* there is an unusual and quite good recipe for a crustless corn tart. The recipe comes from Guadalajara, he says, and he suggests serving it with fried chicken or for breakfast with grilled ham and maple syrup.

I serve it with his recipe for fried chicken, and the combination of the flavors of the two is excellent. Served as a savory I think the sugar could be reduced some, but for breakfast, the recipe should absolutely remain the same.

If at all possible, use fresh corn, but if not, frozen will suffice.

FRESH CORN TART

2 tablespoons bread crumbs
1-1/2 cups fresh corn (about 3 large
 ears cut from the cob)
1 teaspoon salt
1/4 cup granulated sugar
2 tablespoons butter, melted
3 eggs, separated
2 tablespoons all-purpose flour
1/2 cup whipping cream
3/4 cup milk
1 teaspoon pure vanilla extract
freshly ground pepper

Preheat oven to 400 degrees.

Grease a 1-quart souffle dish and dust with bread crumbs.

Combine the corn, salt, sugar, and butter; mix well. Beat the egg yolks and the flour in a large bowl until smooth; stir in the cream, milk, and vanilla. Pour into the prepared souffle dish. Sprinkle with fresh pepper.

Bake 20 minutes. Reduce heat to 375 degrees; bake until a toothpick inserted in center of tart comes out fairly clean, 35 to 40 minutes.

•

When Greg Reynolds, chef of the Dynamite Mousse Company, prepared *Fresh Tuna Grenobleoise*, people often complained that although it was good, it was too acidic. I mentioned to him in conversation that I had found vanilla really helped to cut acidity in fruits and sauces. This led him to experiment by adding vanilla to the sauce. It mellowed the sauce and brought up the flavor of the tuna. Excellent.

FRESH TUNA GRENOBLEOISE WITH VANILLA

4 6- to 8-ounce fillets of tuna
2 tablespoons capers
2 teaspons pure vanilla extract
2 lemons, sectioned, membrane
 removed
1/2 cup white wine
1 tablespoon shallots, minced
1/4 teaspoon garlic, minced
4 tablespoons clarified butter
Worcestershire sauce
flour
salt and pepper

Moisten the fish fillets with Worcestershire, then dust in flour. Heat clarified butter in a large saucepan and add fish fillets, cooking just until done. Remove fillets and place on platter in warm oven.

Add shallots to pan and saute until golden. Add garlic and capers and cook for another minute. Add remaining ingredients and cook until wine has partially evaporated. Season to taste, pour over fish, and serve.

•

This delicious dish confirms that seafood and vanilla are well matched.

SCALLOPS PAIMPOL

4 tablespoons butter
2 tablespoons vanilla flavored
  olive oil
1 medium sized onion, chopped
4 shallots or scallions
1/2 pound mushrooms, finely
  chopped
3 tablespoons flour
2 pounds scallops
2 cups white wine
1/2 vanilla bean
1 tablespoon parsley, finely chopped
2 tablespoons sherry or white wine
2 tablespoons lemon juice
2 tablespoons whipping cream or
  creme fraiche
breadcrumbs

Preheat oven to 450 degrees.

Heat 2 tablespoons butter with olive oil in a saucepan and saute onion, 2 shallots, and mushrooms. Add a little salt and pepper when mixture is lightly browned, then cook over high heat until the moisture has evaporated. Spread the mushrooms on the bottom and sides of scallop shells, or in ramekins.

Cook scallops in 2 cups of white wine and vanilla bean for about 10 minutes, or until done. Remove vanilla bean, strain liquor, saving it, and slice scallops.

Saute 2 shallots in 2 tablespoons butter for about 5 minutes, not allowing them to brown.

Stir in 3 tablespoons flour and continue to stir until the mixture is smooth. Then add hot scallop liquor and cook, stirring constantly, until the sauce is thickened.

Add scallops, parsley, sherry, and salt to taste. Let the mixture cook gently for 5 minutes. Place the scallops on top of the mushrooms, mounding them in the center. Add lemon juice and cream to the sauce then spread it evenly over the scallops in the shells.

Sprinkle with bread crumbs, dot with butter, and bake for about 8 minutes or until the tops are browned.

●

MUSSELS, SHRIMP, AND SOLE VANILLA

6 fillets of sole
1-1/2 cups white wine
1-1/2 cups fish stock
  (or chicken broth)
6 tablespoons unsalted butter
2 shallots, finely chopped
1/2 vanilla bean, split lengthwise
2 dozen mussels
2 dozen shrimp
2 dozen mushroom caps cooked
  in 2 tablespoons butter
juice of 1 lemon
3 tablespoons bechamel sauce
  for fish
2 tablespoons whipped cream

Poach sole for about 10 minutes in wine and fish stock which have been lightly salted and contain vanilla bean, chopped shallots, and butter.

Remove fillets to a flameproof serving dish, remove vanilla bean, then reduce liquid by 2/3 by cooking over high heat. Add *Bechamel Sauce* (see recipe below) and 3 tablespoons butter. Stir until the butter is melted; then strain the sauce.

Arrange around the fish fillets the mussels and shrimps, cooked and drained, and the mushroom caps. Pour lemon juice over all. Fold 2 tablespoons whipped cream into the sauce, pour over the fillets, and glaze the sauce briefly under the broiler.

Bechamel Sauce Maigre:

1/4 cup butter
1/2 onion, finely minced
1/4 cup flour
3 cups scalded milk
3 cups fish stock
1/2 teaspoon salt
pepper to taste
parsley sprig
pinch of freshly grated nutmeg

In a saucepan saute butter and onion over low heat until it is soft but not browned. Stir in 1/4 cup flour and cook slowly for a few minutes. Gradually add scalded milk and fish stock, stirring vigorously with a wire whip. Add parsley, salt, pepper and nutmeg.

Cook slowly, stirring frequently, for about 30 minutes, or until the liquid is reduced by 1/3 and the sauce has the consistency of heavy cream. Strain and dot with butter to keep film from forming on top. Freeze unused sauce for another meal.

•

CRAB STUFFED HALIBUT STEAKS

2 halibut or other firm fleshed fish steaks, about 3 pounds total weight
4 tablespoons butter, melted
1 cup soft bread crumbs
1 onion, chopped
2 tablespoons vanilla flavored olive oil
1 cup cooked crab meat
2 eggs, beaten
1 tablespoon parsley, finely chopped
salt and freshly ground white pepper to taste
up to 1 teaspoon pure vanilla extract (to taste)
2 tablespoons dry white wine or sauterne
juice of 1/2 lemon
1 cup cream or creme fraiche

Preheat oven to 400 degrees.

Saute onion in olive oil.

Brush halibut steaks with melted butter, and sprinkle with salt and pepper. Lay one steak in a buttered baking dish.

Mix bread crumbs, onion, crab meat, eggs, parsley, wine, and vanilla. Add up to 2 tablespoons of butter. Spread this mixture over first steak, and then top with second steak. Sprinkle with lemon juice. Add 1 cup heavy cream and add remaining butter, if any.

Bake for 35 to 40 minutes, or until flesh flakes easily. If the fish begins to brown too much, cover with buttered parchment paper.

•

This is a very pretty dish, delicate and delicious. A nice special entree to serve for friends or family.

CORNISH GAME HENS WITH CHERRIES AND VANILLA

4 cups fresh or canned cherries
1/2 cup kirsch
1/2 cup water (or juice from can)
1 vanilla bean, split
6 small game hens
salt and pepper
butter

Pit cherries and tie the pits into a cheesecloth bag. Put cherries, pits, kirsch, water, and vanilla bean into a saucepan. Bring liquid to a boil and simmer the cherries gently for several minutes until they are tender.

Season game hens with salt and pepper, place in roasting pan, and dot generously with butter. Roast in oven until done, basting frequently, and adding more butter if necessary.

Arrange game hens on platter. Discard cherry pits, remove vanilla bean, and pour cherries and juice into the pan in which the birds were sauteed. Bring to a boil, stirring, and pour sauce and cherries over birds.

Garnish with parsley if desired.

•

Apple *Schnapps* or even cider can be substituted for *Calvados* if desired.

CHICKEN WITH CALVADOS AND VANILLA

2 2-pound chickens, cut into serving
pieces
1/2 cup clarified butter (or 1/4 cup
each olive oil and butter)
1/4 cup warm Calvados or
apple Schnapps
5 shallots, finely chopped
1 tablespoon parsley, chopped
1 sprig of thyme (1/4 teaspoon
dried thyme)
1/2 cup apple cider or white wine
1/2 vanilla bean, split
1/2 cup heavy cream

Brown chicken in butter or oil-butter mixture. Lower heat and cook the pieces 15 minutes longer, turning them often. Add warm *Calvados* or apple *Schnapps* and ignite (or turn heat to high and cook off), shaking pan until the flame dies.

Add shallots, parsley, thyme, cider, or wine, and vanilla bean. Blend the sauce well, cover the pan, and cook the chicken until it is tender.

Remove the chicken from sauce and place on warm platter. Remove the vanilla bean. Add 1/2 cup heavy cream to the sauce, and heat without boiling. Pour the sauce over the chicken just before serving.

•

There is no doubt in my mind that if vanilla had been available to the Indians it would have been used in myriad ways, most especially in curries.

CURRIED CHICKEN WITH VANILLA

2 cups coconut milk (unsweetened)
  or 1 small coconut and 2 cups milk
3 tablespoons vanilla flavored
  olive oil
1 onion, chopped
2 tablespoons ginger root, chopped
  or minced
1 clove garlic
3 tablespoons flour
1/2 teaspoon cinnamon
2 teaspoons curry powder
2 teaspoons sugar
1 teaspoon pure vanilla extract
3- to 4-pounds chicken meat,
  cooked, boned, and cut into
  2 inch pieces

If using fresh coconut, grate the meat into a bowl, and add 1 cup hot milk; let set for 10 minutes then squeeze the coconut through cheesecloth, reserving the coconut milk. Repeat with another cup of hot milk.

Saute onion, ginger root, and garlic in butter and oil. Stir in flour, cinnamon, sugar and curry powder, and continue to cook gently, stirring until the sauce is thickened. Add vanilla extract.

Just before serving, add chicken and adjust salt and pepper seasonings. Serve with rice and condiments.

Suggested condiments: quartered limes, toasted grated coconut, chutney, fresh pineapple, and almonds.

•

At the beginning of the 18th century Louis La Griffe wrote, "Vanilla became associated with chocolate, the vanilla being held to increase the aphrodisiac and anti-venereal disease properties of the chocolate." (It would seem from the quantity of vanilla-laced chocolate consumed in our culture that we should be a sex-crazed society—but a lot healthier than we are!)

Chef Philip Farar of *Noveau Classique* chose veal for the entree of a complete meal based on vanilla. This recipe is for two; double it if you wish, or make it as part of a very romantic meal for two. Serve oysters for a first course, this for a second, and fresh fruit and a vanilla cream for the perfect seductive meal.

VEAL WITH VANILLA AND PERNOD

8 ounces veal cutlets, pounded
1 large vanilla bean
1 bunch spinach, washed well
 and drained
1 cup pearl onions, peeled
2 tablespoons olive oil
1 tablespoon butter
4 ounces champagne
2 ounces Pernod
1/2 cup flour
1 teaspoon garlic, minced
salt to taste

Flour the veal and set aside. Saute half of the vanilla bean and all the garlic with olive in a heavy frying pan. When the pan is very hot, lightly brown the veal on each side (about 20 to 30 seconds per side). Remove the veal from pan and set aside, keeping warm.

Add onions, butter, and heavy cream to pan. Reduce the liquid by one-third, stirring frequently. When the sauce has reduced, add veal and Pernod and simmer about 1 minute more.

While the sauce is reducing, heat the champagne to boiling point. Poach the spinach until just tender (1 to 3 minutes). Drain. Place spinach on a platter, forming a bed for the veal. Place the veal on the spinach, leaving a ring of green around the veal.

Ladle the sauce over the center of the veal. Place onions on the spinach ring, surrounding veal.

Scrape the seeds of the remaining vanilla bean over the dish and serve.

•

Ham is a natural for vanilla. Traditionally served with fruits, the vanilla will accentuate the flavors. Put a little vanilla extract into your favorite glazes or toppings when you next prepare pork or ham.

HAM WITH PEACHES AND VANILLA

1/2 cup water
2 tablespoons sugar
4 cloves
1 cinnamon stick
1 vanilla bean or 1-1/2 teaspoons
 pure vanilla extract
3 cups peaches, sliced
1 tablespoon cornstarch mixed with
 2 tablespoons water
2 cooked ham steaks, 3/4-inch thick

Preheat oven to 350 degrees.

Combine water, sugar, cloves, cinnamon, and vanilla bean in a saucepan. Bring the mixture to a boil and add sliced peaches. Simmer gently for 5 minutes, then add cornstarch and water. Cook, stirring constantly, until the sauce is clear.

Place the ham steaks in a lightly buttered baking dish. Pour the sauce over the ham and bake the ham for 30 minutes (or until well cooked), basting frequently.

Transfer ham to serving plate, remove cloves, cinnamon, and vanilla bean, and pour remaining sauce over ham steaks.

•

When I first asked various chefs and friends whom I knew enjoyed cooking if they had a favorite recipe that included vanilla as a focal point, or if they would be willing to experiment with vanilla, Verena La Mar, of the Dynamite Mousse Catering Service told me of a Swiss recipe her family was quite fond of. When she wrote the recipe down for me I asked her what "Hali Hula" meant. She wasn't really certain—perhaps it was the restaurant's idea of something that sounded Hawaiian.

Whatever the name means, the recipe was provided for us by her father, Hermann Gfeller who was out the evening she called, eating Hali Hula at the Belpmoos Airport Restaurant in Bern, Switzerland.

HALI HULA

1-1/2 cups rice
3 cups water
1 teaspoon salt
1-1/2 pounds of very thinly sliced chicken breast, veal, or flank steak cut in 2-inch lengths
3 tablespoons flour
salt and white pepper to taste
1 tablespoon curry powder (or to taste)
8 tablespoons butter
1-1/2 cups whipping cream

Fruits:

4 pineapple slices
4 peach halves
1 banana, sliced lengthwise and cut in half
4 apricot halves
some maraschino cherries for color
2 tablespoons butter
1 tablespoon and 1 teaspoon pure vanilla extract
2 cups whipping cream
1 tablespoon sugar

Cook rice in salted water until dry and fluffy. Keep warm.

Mix flour, salt, and pepper in a plastic bag. Add chicken or meat, and shake to coat evenly.

Melt 4 tablespoons of the butter until clear and hot. Add meat and saute quickly, about 3 minutes. Remove from pan and keep warm.

Add the remaining butter and curry powder. Cook until fragrant and creamy. Add heavy cream. Stir well until the mixture is smooth and the back of the spoon is lightly coated. Add the meat and juices, and keep warm.

In a separate frying pan, melt 2 tablespoons butter. Saute fruits very quickly in the butter, just until they are warm. Add vanilla, turn off heat, and let sit covered for about 2 minutes.

Whip 2 cups whipping cream. Add vanilla and sugar and continue whipping until there are soft peaks. Place cream in small bowl.

To serve, place rice on a large platter that has been warmed. Pour curry over rice. Place fruits around the curry dish, and serve cream on the side. Serves 4 to 6.

•

When the Mogols invaded India during the 16th century, their central Asian Muslim cuisine, which is based on meat, was brought to northern and central India, to the Punjab. This is why meat dishes are more likely found in this region than in the south.

Additionally, because the Punjabi people use wheat, rather than rice, as a staple in their diet, the food is dryer and the sauces thicker than farther south, where the rice absorbs the juices of the foods. The food is eaten with *chapatis,* flat, unleavened whole-wheat bread and with fingers rather than utensils.

This explains why a lamb and spinach dish which is very central Asian in character is found in the Punjab. The vanilla is *not* traditionally found in either cuisine. I have the feeling, however, that if vanilla had been available to the Indians, it would have been incorporated very quickly into their cuisine.

LAMB WITH SPINACH FROM THE PUNJAB

3 pounds lean lamb, cut in 2-1/2-inch cubes
1-1/2 pounds spinach, cut in 1/4-inch strips
3 onions, thinly sliced
6 tablespoons clarified butter
1 vanilla bean, split down center
1-1/2 teaspoons ground turmeric
1 tablespoon coriander seed
4 teaspoons ground ginger
3/4 teaspoon chili powder (or to taste)
3 tablespoons yogurt
1/4 teaspoon thyme
4 teaspoons mustard seed
salt to taste

Saute onions in butter. Add meat, vanilla bean, turmeric, coriander, ginger, and chili powder and simmer for 10 minutes. Stir in spinach, yogurt, thyme, mustard seeds, and salt. Cover and simmer for 15 minutes, stirring occasionally. Add 1/4 cup water and simmer for 15 minutes. Before serving, remove vanilla bean.

This dish can be prepared a day ahead and warmed before serving. Having a few hours to allow the flavors to mellow makes it richer. Serve with *chapatis* or flour tortillas, or over rice. Condiments can be served on the side if desired. Serves 6.

The word *mole* comes from the Nahuatl, *molli,* sauce. Although the *Mole Poblano de Guajalote* has sometimes been credited to Sor Andrea, Sister Superior of the San Rosa Convent in Puebla, it is much more likely a pre-Columbian dish. Because this mole has chocolate in it, it would have been a dish for Aztec royalty. Instead of cloves and cinnamon, allspice would have been used.

The Aztecs used vanilla in savory dishes. Vanilla was not listed as an ingredient for this mole, but it seemed to me that as vanilla is so effective with chocolate, that it would be good in this dish. And in fact, it is. The flavor is very subtle, but it definitely lends a delicate quality to this entree.

MOLE POBLANA DE GUAJALOTE

6 ancho chili peppers
2 pasilla chili peppers
6 mulato chili peppers
8 pounds turkey, cut into serving
    pieces
1 vanilla bean, split
salt
8 tablespoons clarified butter
2 medium-sized onions, chopped
3 garlic cloves, chopped
1/4 teaspoon anise seeds
1/4 teaspoon cloves
1/2 teaspoon cinnamon
6 tablespoons sesame seeds
1 cup blanched almonds, chopped
1/2 cup seedless raisins
1 pound tomatoes, blanched,
    peeled, seeded and chopped
2 stale 4-inch tortillas
2 ounces unsweetened chocolate
2 teaspoons pure vanilla extract

Remove the stems from the chilies, shake out and discard the seeds. Tear the chilies into pieces and put them to soak in 2 cups of hot water.

Place the turkey pieces in a large casserole, cover with salted water, and add vanilla bean. Bring to a boil and simmer for 1 hour. Drain, reserving the stock. Rinse and dry the casserole.

Dry turkey pieces with paper towels. Brown the turkey in butter, in a large frying pan, a few pieces at a time. Transfer the turkey pieces to the casserole. Reserve butter.

In a food processor or blender, puree the chilies, the water in which they were soaked, onions, garlic, anise seeds, cloves, cinnamon, 4 tablespoons of the sesame seeds, almonds, raisins, tomatoes, and tortillas. This should be done in several batches; do not overblend. The puree should be heavy and coarse.

Reheat the butter and cook the chili mixture, stirring constantly, for 5 minutes. Add 2 cups of the turkey broth, chocolate, and salt to taste and cook, stirring, until the chocolate has melted. Add vanilla extract.

Pour the sauce over the turkey pieces. Cover the casserole and simmer very gently for 30 minutes.

Cook the remaining sesame seeds in a frying pan or toast in the oven. Sprinkle them over the mole just before serving. Serves 8 to 10.

●

8
SAUCES, SYRUPS & TOPPINGS

Savory Sauces and Dressings

After having a conversation with Greg Reynolds, chef of the Dynamite Mousse Company, about where and how vanilla is grown, he began playing around with ideas of how he could represent Madagascar in a sauce for meats. He said that suddenly he made an association of green peppercorns connected with Madagascar, and he felt that the sweetness in the vanilla would balance well with the pungent bite of peppercorns. The resulting sauce is excellent on any cut of beef. He made it for me on steak, but it would be excellent on roasts or veal fillets or medallions of beef. It would also be quite good as a fondue sauce using thin slices of beef and French bread. Mushrooms can be added to this sauce.

SAUCE MADAGASCAR (GREEN PEPPERCORN AND VANILLA)

1/2 cup brandy
2 vanilla beans, chopped
1 cup brown sauce or demi-glaze
1 tablespoon green Madagascar
  peppercorns
dash of Worcestershire
2 tablespoons clarified butter
1 tablespoon chopped shallots
1/4 teaspoon chopped garlic
1 tablespoon heavy cream
salt and pepper to taste

Heat brandy and vanilla together in a frying pan and bring to boil. Drop heat slightly and allow to simmer until mixture is reduced by half. Set aside.

So strong and effective is the perfume of vanilla, that 1 ground vanilla bean is considered sufficient for flavoring 1½ pounds of chocolate.

Saute shallots in 2 tablespoons clarified butter. Add green peppercorns and garlic, and cook until all are carmelized.

Pour the brandy-vanilla mixture back into the pan, first removing vanilla beans. Add the cream, salt and pepper to taste.

This sauce can be made up several hours in advance of preparing meat. It is wise to make it the same day it is to be served, however, as the peppercorns will make the sauce too spicy if allowed to steep in the sauce for too long.

•

This glaze is another of Greg Reynolds' marvellous sauces. This one he made to go with lamb but it really is good for any meats, for fish, and even for tofu. Apply the glaze before roasting, smoking, or cooking on a barbeque. Large mushrooms could be glazed and cooked at the last minute to go with the meat.

VANILLA GLAZE FOR MEATS, POULTRY, AND FOWL

1/2 cup red wine vinegar
1/2 cup sugar
1/2 cup madeira
1 cup water or stock
2 vanilla beans, chopped
2 tablespoons cornstarch
3 tablespoons water

In a medium-heavy saucepan, bring red wine vinegar and sugar to a boil. Continue cooking for about 10 to 15 minutes or until sugar has carmelized. Watch carefully as sugar burns easily. When carmelized, add madeira and stir until sugar mixture has dissolved.

Add stock or water and vanilla beans, and simmer on stove until the mixture has reduced by one half. Remove from heat and let stand for at least one hour.

When ready to use, remove vanilla beans and then reheat mixture, bringing it to a simmer. Mix 2 tablespoons cornstarch with water and add to sauce. Simmer 3 minutes or until thick. Glaze meat before cooking and add as needed.

Makes about 1-1/2 cups sauce.

•

Philip Farar, chef of Noveau Classique, created a meal incorporating vanilla into each course. The Vanilla Macadamia Nut Dressing could be served over mixed greens or a lettuce and vegetable salad.

VANILLA-MACADAMIA NUT DRESSING

1 large vanilla bean, chopped
6 to 8 ounces Macadamia nuts
8 ounces walnut oil
5 ounces raspberry vinegar
1 shallot
1/2 teaspoon coriander
2 strips lemon zest
1 teaspoon fresh ginger
1-1/2 teaspoons sugar
salt to taste

Combine ingredients in a blender and whip until smooth. Strain into a jar, and refrigerate until ready to use.

•

The Hollandaise sauce recipe that follows is one that I've used for years. I like it because it is almost "no-fail," and it also uses whole eggs. The difference with this sauce now is that I added a few drops of pure vanilla extract after hearing that vanilla softens the "bite" in acidic foods. I liked how it smoothed the sauce, and will continue to add a few drops of vanilla in the future.

HOLLANDAISE SAUCE

8 tablespoons butter
juice of 1 lemon
2 eggs
a few drops of pure vanilla extract
salt and pepper to taste
1 tablespoon hot water

In a heavy 1-quart saucepan, melt butter. Add the lemon juice and water.

In a small bowl beat eggs with a whisk, add a few drops of vanilla extract, then slowly pour into the butter-lemon mixture, stirring constantly with whisk.

As soon as sauce begins to thicken, turn off heat, beating until thick. Add salt and pepper to taste.

This sauce can be made an hour ahead and warmed to serve. Add a few drops of hot water when warming. If the sauce should curdle, it can be saved by adding a tablespoon of hot water and beating with a whisk as it is warmed over low heat.

•

Bernaise sauce is a variation of sorts on Hollandaise. I added the vanilla for the same reason, had the same results, and am passing it on to you. If the Bernaise should curdle, follow the same instructions as with the Hollandaise.

BERNAISE SAUCE

1/4 cup wine vinegar or
dry white vermouth
1 tablespoon shallots, minced
(or green onions, minced)
3 tablespoons fresh tarragon,
minced (or 1 tablespoon tarragon
and 2 tablespoons parsley, minced)
1/8 teaspoon white pepper
1/3 cup butter
2 whole eggs
a few drops of pure vanilla extract
pinch of salt

In a heavy 1-quart saucepan, boil vinegar (or vermouth) with shallots (or green onions), 1 tablespoon tarragon (or you may substitute 1/2 tablespoon of dried tarragon leaves), pepper and a pinch of salt.

Pour off and discard all but 2 tablespoons of this boiled mixture.

In the same saucepan, melt butter.

Beat eggs, add a dash of vanilla, and add to melted butter. Add 2 tablespoons tarragon or parsley. Beat until thick with a whisk.

Remove from heat as soon as thickened.

•

Sweet Sauces and Toppings

This is basically a simple syrup that can be used to mix with fruits, cover waffles or pancakes, glaze a ham, provide the base for liqueurs—or fill in for any recipe that calls for a sugar syrup.

VANILLA SYRUP

3/4 cup sugar
2 cups water
dash of salt (optional)
1 vanilla bean, split but intact

Combine the sugar, water, salt, and vanilla bean in a 1-quart saucepan and mix well. Bring to the boiling point and boil 2 minutes. Remove the vanilla bean, and add pure vanilla extract to taste if a richer vanilla flavor is desired. Makes 2-1/4 cups.

Nearly 2 million pounds of vanilla beans were imported into the United States in 1985. Most of the beans were converted into vanilla extract for home use and for use as a flavoring component in the food and beverage industries.

The last survey on the use of vanillin showed that just over 1 million pounds were used in 1980. If vanilla beans had been substituted for the vanillin, 50 million pounds of beans would have been necessary.

Philip Farar used as his dessert fresh fruits with a vanilla Sabayon. Although Sabayon could be classified under custard sauces as it is similar to *Creme Anglaise,* I decided to place it with the sauces and toppings as it is more like a sauce to be poured over fruits or steamed puddings. It is rich, silky, and delicious!

VANILLA SABAYON

5 large egg yolks
2-1/2 ounces butter
2 ounces Grand Marnier
2 teaspoons pure vanilla extract
1-1/2 teaspoons sugar
4 ounces heavy cream

Heat yolks in a double boiler, whisking until thick and slightly darkened in color. Melt butter in a separate saucepan and combine with the eggs, about 2 teaspoons at a time. Continue whisking until it becomes the consistency of mayonnaise.

Combine remaining ingredients in a bowl with the heavy cream, and whip until fluffy. Slowly add the cream mixture into the egg mixture, whipping until the sauce is thick and creamy but not stiff.

•

This is similar to the Sabayon sauce except that it depends on the cornstarch for thickening instead of the egg yolks. It is a little less tricky to have turn out without curdling; if you haven't much experience making creams, you might feel a little safer with this recipe for a first go at it.

VANILLA CREAM SAUCE

1/4 cup sugar
2 teaspoons cornstarch
1 vanilla bean, split but intact
pinch of salt
2 large egg yoks, lightly beaten
1-1/2 cups milk or light cream
1 teaspoon pure vanilla extract
1/2 cup heavy cream, whipped

Combine sugar, cornstarch, vanillla bean, and salt in a heavy medium saucepan or in the top of a double boiler. Add egg yolks and mix well. Stir in the milk.

Cook, stirring constantly, over low heat or over hot water until the custard coats a metal spoon. Remove the heat and cool completely. Fold in vanilla extract and whipped cream.

Makes approximately 2-1/2 cups.

•

VANILLA CHIFFON SAUCE

1/3 cup butter, softened
1-1/2 cups sifted vanilla
    confectioners sugar
1 egg, separated
2 teaspoons pure vanilla extract
1/2 cup heavy cream
1/8 teaspoon ground nutmeg

In a small mixing bowl, cream butter with sugar, egg yolk and vanilla extract; blend well. Beat cream until stiff; fold into butter mixture (sauce will be foamy). Sprinkle with nutmeg and serve over fruitcake, steamed puddings, or sponge cake.

•

Cultured creams have been around forever. The French use Creme Fraiche, the British, clotted cream, and the Americans, sour cream. Creme Fraiche is not quite as tart as sour cream, but more tart than plain cream.

CREME FRAICHE VANILLA

1 cup cream
1/2 cup sour cream
1 tablespoon pure vanilla extract
1 tablespoon sugar

Combine cream and sour cream in a jar with a tight fitting lid, and keep in a warm, draft-free place for about 8 hours. Add sugar and vanilla,and allow to sit another few hours until thick. Refrigerate until ready to use.

•

The following is a quick version of *creme fraiche* that can be used as a substitute if necessary.

ERSATZ
CREME FRAICHE VANILLA

4 ounces cream cheese,
room temperature
1 cup sour cream
1 cup heavy cream
1 teaspoon vanilla sugar
(or more, to taste)
1 tablespoon pure vanilla extract

Place all ingredients in blender or food processor, and blend until smooth.

•

When I was growing up my father occasionally used to buy peppermint ice cream and butterscotch sauce and bring it home for dessert. Because he seemed to enjoy it, I learned to enjoy it. Years later he told me he didn't really remember buying peppermint ice cream and butterscotch sauce, and he didn't think he would like the combination. I can now honestly say I'm not real big on peppermint ice cream, and never was, but I do very much enjoy butterscotch sauce. This is a good recipe. Try it on one of the vanilla ice cream recipes.

BUTTERSCOTCH SAUCE

1/2 cup light corn syrup
1 cup brown sugar
2 ounces unsalted butter
1 tablespoon pure vanilla extract
3/4 cup heavy cream

In a heavy saucepan, bring the corn syrup, brown sugar, and butter to a boil. Boil gently for about 5 minutes, stirring occasionally, until mixture is 235 degrees on a candy thermometer. Remove from heat, add the vanilla, and stir vigorously for 1 minute with a whip.

Let mixture cool to warm. Add the heavy cream, a little at a time, beating with whip after each addition. The mixture will become smooth and shiny. Pour the sauce into a clean jar, and keep in the refrigerator. It will keep for several months.

To serve, heat sauce over warm water. Makes about 3 cups.

•

9
SOME ADDITIONAL NOTES & RECIPES

There were a number of recipes for this collection that didn't fit into any specific category and so they have been relegated to the somewhat dubious position of being miscellaneous.

But these recipes—both edible and non-edible—are varied, unusual, and quite good.

Cortes apparently felt that vanilla enhanced coffee in the same way it enhanced chocolate. He advised the royal chefs of Spain to put equal parts of vanilla pods and coffee beans together, roast, and prepare for the King as an evening drink. He felt this mixture would provide a sound sleep without "horrid dreams." His advice was not taken; it was felt that vanilla pods were too expensive to use this way—even for the king.

About twenty years ago, a friend who was very influential in educating me in the ways of European and eclectic cooking, told me to purchase vanilla beans at the same small store in San Francisco where I bought my fresh coffee beans. He told me to keep my vanilla bean stored in with the coffee beans, and when I had ground the coffee and placed it in the filter (I use a Brazil bag—a reusable cloth bag with a wire rim around the top—placed over my coffee pot), to put the vanilla bean in as well, and to allow the hot water to pour over it.

This, he said, would make the coffee much more palatable (and I think he hinted at "mysterious"). I have never drunk coffee, so I can't tell you if it was either better or more mysterious, but I liked the ritual, and my guests asked for more. Try it for a special treat; you may also be able to expunge any "horrid dreams," assuming you can get to sleep after drinking coffee in the evening.

The old roundup cooks travelling with the cowboys used to hide their bottles of 70 proof vanilla extract, and they kept an eye on their provisions at all times lest the thirsty cowboy should get a hankerin' for a little free spirit.

Like most rare and unusual foods, herbs, and spices, vanilla has been considered valuable for many different ailments over the years. It was, of course, at one time considered an aphrodisiac, not only in Europe, but by the Indians as well. It was even more valued for the Pharmacopoeia of the United States up until the 1916 edition when it was eliminated in favor of other medications. A few pharmacies still make or carry small-label pure vanilla extracts.

The following recipe is from an English herbal book. It is meant to be taken before meals to aid in digestion and to calm the stomach.

TARRAGON-VANILLA DIGESTIVE

4 sprigs French tarragon
1 vanilla pod, split down the center
2-1/2 cups brandy

Steep the above ingredients together for a fortnight (two weeks), strain, and place in a bottle. Take a tablespoon of this digestive before meals.

•

This healthful and unusual recipe is from the *Sea Vegetable Gourmet Cookbook and Foragers Guide*, written by John and Eleanor Lewallen. John and Eleanor and family live in Mendocino County and have a business gathering, packaging, and selling seaweeds, which are extremely high in protein, vitamins A and C, and trace minerals. When I mentioned to Eleanor that I was working on a book on vanilla, she sent this recipe which she makes frequently for her children.

If you have never tried nori, don't be put off by your imagination. It is delicately flavored, and actually quite good as well as being healthful. This recipe, however, could be made without the nori if you prefer.

ELEANOR LEWALLEN'S FESTIVE POPCORN

1 quart popcorn, popped
(3/4 cup kernels)
1 cup loosely packed wild nori,
or 2 sheets nori*
1/4 cube butter or margarine
1-1/2 teaspoons pure vanilla extract
2 to 3 tablespoons honey
1 tablespoon molasses
1 to 2 tablespoons
powdered cinnamon

*Nori can be found in Oriental grocery stores and health food stores.

Place wild nori or nori in sheets in the oven or on top of the stove in a skillet for about 2 minutes, toasting very lightly. Nori is delicate, so don't overtoast.

Flake nori into a bowl with popcorn, gently crumbling it with your fingers.

In a saucepan, add honey, molasses, butter, and vanilla. Stir until completely melted. Add cinnamon to taste. Pour over popcorn-nori mixture tossing lightly with a fork or spoon to cover kernels.

•

The grains in granola are definitely enhanced by vanilla. Fructose, date sugar, or maple sugar can be substituted for the brown sugar. If using fructose, reduce quantity slightly.

VANILLA GRANOLA

4 cups rolled oats
2 cups wheat germ
1 cup shredded, unsweetened
   coconut
1 cup chopped nuts
1 cup sesame seeds
1/2 cup firmly packed brown sugar
3/4 cup oil (safflower or sunflower
   are nice, light oils)
3/4 cup water
2 tablespoons pure vanilla extract

Preheat oven to 325 degrees.

Mix oats, wheat germ, coconut, nuts, sesame seeds, and brown sugar until well blended. Combine oil, water, and vanilla and pour over dry ingredients; mix very well. Place in a shallow roasting or broiling pan.

Bake 1 hour, stirring every 15 minutes. When done, granola should be a dark golden brown. Store in jars or other airtight containers.

•

This recipe comes from the *Nut Lovers' Cookbook,* by Shirl Carder. The flavor is reminiscent of a raw sugar candy made with orange peel, cinnamon, and vanilla.

PENUCHE NUTS

1 cup firmly packed brown sugar
1/2 teaspoon salt
1/2 teaspoon cinnamon
6 tablespoons milk
1 teaspoon pure vanilla extract
1 teaspooon grated orange peel
3 cups nut halves

In a saucepan combine sugar, cinnamon, and milk; stir to blend. Cook, stirring occasionally, until mixture reaches 236 degrees on a candy thermometer.

Remove from heat and stir in vanilla, orange peel, and nuts. Continue stirring until mixture begins to lose its gloss and a coating forms on the nuts.

Turn mixture onto brown paper. Using two forks, separate nuts. Cool completely and store covered. Makes 3-1/2 cups.

Louis La Griffe wrote in Le Livre des Epices, des Condiments et des aromates, *"Vanilla is not strictly speaking, either a spice or a seasoner; it would seem more exact to call it a perfume."*

This recipe is also from the *Nut Lovers Cookbook*. Shirl Carder comments that this is a nice gift for people who "have everything."

CARAMEL NUTS

1 cup firmly packed brown sugar
1/2 cup vanilla sugar
1/2 cup half-and-half
2 tablespoons light corn syrup
1 tablespoon butter
1 tablespoon pure vanilla extract
2 cups nut halves

Combine sugars, half-and-half, and corn syrup in a saucepan. Cook until a little syrup dropped in a cup of cold water forms a soft ball (or 236 on a candy thermometer).

Add nuts and stir until well coated. Turn out onto foil. Separate nuts with two forks. Let stand until cool and firm. Makes 3 cups.

•

Last summer I had some apricots that weren't quite up to flavor. On a whim I put some vanilla extract into the jam just as it was ready to be placed in the jars. On opening a jar of the jam a few weeks later, I found that the vanilla gave the jam the lift that it needed to make it fresh and fruity-flavored.

I recommend adding vanilla —either a bean to the jam as it cooks, or some extract at the end. The following recipe incorporates vanilla as one of the major components of the jam. Morello cherries are a tart variety of cherry; any tart cherry will do as well.

MORELLO CHERRY AND VANILLA JAM

3-1/2 cups vanilla sugar
1 vanilla bean
3 pounds morello cherries
  (or other tart variety)
juice of 2 lemons

Dissolve the sugar in 1-1/4 cups of water over a low heat, then bring to a boil. Add the vanilla bean and the cherries. (The cherries can be pitted or not. If the cherries are pitted, bruise the pits with a hammer, and add to the mixture in a muslin bag.)

Boil for 15 minutes, then leave to cool overnight. The following day add the lemon juice and boil until jam becomes somewhat thickened. Remove the bag of pits and vanilla bean, pour the jam into warm jars, seal, and cover.

•

Crystallized flowers and leaves make a beautiful decoration for cakes, tortes, and mousses. They also are a welcome gift to bakers. The delicate scent of the vanilla enhances the natural scents of the flowers and mint. Homemade flowers and leaves are much more delicate and beautiful than the purchased ones which are usually dyed and often lumpy. And yes, it is okay to eat them—they're quite delicious.

CRYSTALLIZED VIOLETS, ROSEBUDS, ROSE PETALS, AND MINT LEAVES

freshly picked violets, with
stems left on
freshly gathered rose petals,
separated
freshly gathered rosebuds with stems
left to about 1/2 inch
fresh mint leaves
egg white of 1 large egg
superfine granulated vanilla sugar

Gather petals, flowers, or mint leaves on a sunny morning after the dew has dried. Do not wash. Gently shake and blow on the petals or leaves to remove any dust.

Beat the egg white until it begins to stiffen. Place the sugar in a saucer.

Holding the flowers or leaves by the stem (hold very end of rose petals), dip it into the egg white. Using a paintbrush, carefully paint the egg-white evenly over the whole surface area, including the back-side. A needle or hair-pin can be used to hold the petals open if necessary. Next, dip the petals or leaves into the sugar, holding areas open if necessary with the needle or pin. Make certain that all surface area is coated.

Place the finished pieces on a cake rack, and snip off stems. Sprinkle a little more sugar over any missed surfaces. Don't let petals, flowers, or steps touch each other, so air can circulate.

Set the rack in a warm place to dry. If there is any likelihood of dust, cover gently with waxed paper. The inside of an oven with a gas pilot is a good place to dry flowers or leaves. It may take several days before they are completely dry and brittle, however, so be certain to remove from oven before using, and don't put back into oven until it is almost completely cooled.

When the flowers or leaves are completely dried, store between pieces of waxed paper in an airtight container. They will keep indefinitely.

•

Another beautiful sugared creation can be made with grapes or raspberries. A bunch of sugared grapes, offset with a scented geranium leaf is a sophisticated decoration for an elegant chocolate torte, or even a steamed pudding. The raspberries make a glittering topping for cheesecakes or cakes. Make ahead so that fruits have at least two hours to dry, but they should be used within a day or two.

SUGARED GRAPES OR RASPBERRIES

1 large bunch green grapes
1 large bunch red grapes
or
1 to 2 baskets raspberries
2 egg whites
superfine granulated vanilla sugar

Cut grapes into small bunches. Using a paintbrush, brush grapes or raspberries with egg whites, beaten until slightly stiffened. Sift sugar over fruits, turning fruits slightly until completely covered. Place on a rack in a warm, dry place until thoroughly dry.

•

A welcome gift to friends during the winter or holiday season, is a spice bag and a jug of good apple cider or a bottle of Burgundy or Bordeaux wine.

SPICE BAGS

6 vanilla beans, cut in halves
6 cinnamon sticks
6 teaspooons juniper berries
  (optional)
6 teaspooons whole cloves
6 tablespoons grated orange peel
18 cardamom pods
3/4 cup blanched almonds
6 6-inch double layers
  of cheesecloth
twine or string
ribbon

In the center of each square, place 2 vanilla bean halves, 1 cinnamon stick, 1 teaspoon cloves, 1 teaspoon juniper berries, 3 cardamom pods, 1 tablespoon grated orange peel, and 2 tablespoons almonds.

Gather up the edges and tie each square into a neat bag with heavy string or twine. Decorate with ribbon. 1 bag is good for up to 1 gallon of wine or cider.

•

As in all endeavors there are moments when things go wrong, such as the time 200 pounds of insufficiently cured vanilla beans arrived from Tahiti. Peter was running the business out of his apartment which had limited space, but the beans needed to be dried about two more weeks to bring up their full flavor. So Peter laid the beans out to dry throughout his apartment. There were beans across the floor, beans on shelves, beans on the couch, the bed, the range top— everywhere! To speed up the drying process, he opened the windows, sending the fragrance of 200 pounds of beans spilling into the Los Angeles basin. People were drawn to the building from blocks around, curious about the beautiful odor. He says it would have been much better to have dried them outside, but if people were drawn to the scent from inside a building, the beans would have been stolen in a moment if he had placed them out in the sun. Vanilla rustling in America? I think not.

From very early times, herbs, spices, and flowers have played an integral part in the lives of people all over the world. The feeling that health and well being has a direct correlation with scents has perpetuated over the ages. In the Middle Ages, the stench in the European cities was apparently overwhelming. People carried pomanders (from the French, *pomme d'ambre,* or "apple of amber") made of *ambergris* combined with other scented ingredients. Those who could not afford *ambergris* used hollowed orange shells or apple shells filled with herbs and spices. Later pomanders were made from silver, gold, or porcelain, and were perforated to allow the scents to emerge. People also carried these scented containers to protect them against the plague. Some people wore small cloth pouches filled with herbs around their necks.

Although we no longer need to cope with the plague, and the stench of the cities may be more from smog than garbage, the pleasure of pot pourri and pomanders remains.

Creating a quality pot pourri is worth taking some time and care, as a good pot pourri can last up to fifty years. Use fresh ingredients; whenever possible gather the leaves and flowers yourself, and make certain that all spices are fresh. The addition of fixatives such as orris root and essential oils, will make the pot pourri more fragrant. Freshly cut or grind the spices for an interesting texture. When the scent begins to fade, revitalize the mixture with a few drops of brandy, flower oil, essential oil, or use some vanilla extract.

The following recipes can be altered to what is available or to your personal preference. These recipes are especially compatible with the use of vanilla pods.

DRY POT POURRI

10 cups rose petals
2-1/2 cups clove carnation petals
2-1/2 cups lemon verbena leaves
2-1/2 cups lavender flowers
1-1/4 cups rosemary flowers
  and leaves
1-1/2 cups sweet marjoram flowers
  and leaves
1/2 cup peppermint leaves
2-1/2 cups mixed flowers such as
  rosebuds, hyssop, violets, etc.

Mix these with your hands then add:

2 ounces chopped orris root
1 tablespoon grated or powdered
  orris root (or 3 tablespoons of
  powdered orris root)
2 vanilla pods, each chopped into
  3 pieces
1 ounce broken dried tangerine
  peel, each piece stuck with a
  clove
1 teaspoon crushed allspice berries
1 teaspoon crushed coriander
3 inches broken cinnamon stick
2 broken bay leaves
1 teaspoon grated nutmeg
2 broken blades of mace
1 tablespoon chopped dried ginger

Mix all together then add a few drops of rosemary oil.

Store for 6 weeks in a dark, tightly stoppered jar so the scents can blend and mature. Stir every few days with a wooden spoon.

Note: If you are gathering some of the petals, flowers, or leaves yourself, do so early on sunny mornings. Dry them carefully away from direct heat, in an airy, shady room. Store in separate airtight containers.

BLOSSOM AND SPICE POT POURRI

6 ounces rosebuds
2 ounces linden flowers
1 ounce orange blossoms
1 ounce blue malva flowers
1 ounce peony flowers
1 ounce sunflowers
1 ounce patchouli herb
1 ounce rosemary leaves
1 ounce sandalwood chips
3 vanilla beans, chopped
15 drops allspice oil
15 drops verbena oil
2 tablespoons orris root powder or
   5 drops orris root oil

Mix together and bottle in airtight containers. Store in a cool dark place, allowing several weeks for scents to blend.

●

LEMON AND SPICE POT POURRI

4 ounces star anise
3 ounces rosehips
2 ounces orange peel
1 ounce allspice berries
1 ounce cardamom pods
1 ounce cloves
1 ounce orris root
1 ounce sandalwood chips
3 vanilla beans, chopped
1 ounce sassafras bark
20 drops lemongrass oil
15 drops rose geranium oil
10 drops frankincense oil
5 drops myrrh oil

Mix as in previous recipes.

If making pot pourri from "scratch" is not for you, there are a large number of prepared blends available. Choose one that would be compatible with vanilla scent, and add chopped vanilla beans to the mixture.

●

A D D E N D U M

ADDENDUM

Sheila Linderman, who works with TAHITIAN IMPORT / EXPORT, INC., has contributed the following three recipes developed specifically for the new edition of this book.

Sheila has an impressive background in the culinary arts. She worked and studied at Peltier and Hardel in Paris. She was a pastry chef at Maple Drive in Beverly Hills; 72 market Street in Venice, California; Le Chardonnay in West Hollywood; and was head baker at Cocolat in San Francisco. She coauthored *Salads* with Leonard Schwartz, authored *Il Fornaio,* and is currently at work on *Dinner at the Authentic Cafe.*

PEAR PRESERVES WITH VANILLA

Fills twelve 8 ounce jars

4-1/2 pounds firm pears
7-1/2 cups sugar
2 cups water
1 lemon (juice and zest)
1 vanilla bean, split lengthwise

Peel and quarter the pears, removing the seeds and cores. As you work, place the pears in a bowl of cool water to keep them from turning brown.

Blanch pears in boiling water for 2 minutes, then drain them.

Combine the sugar with the water and bring to a boil in a large pot. As soon as the mixture starts to boil, add the lemon juice and zest, as well as the vanilla bean. Add the pears and cook over high heat for about 45 minutes, or until quite thick.

Remove the zest and the vanilla bean before filling jars.

These preserves will keep for 1 year if properly sealed.

CONFITURE DE POIRES A LA VANILLE

Pour 12 pots de 250g

2 kg de poires a chair ferme
1.5 kg de sucre
500 ml d'eau
1 citron (zeste et jus)
1 gousse de vanille

Pelez les poires, coupez-les en quartiers en retirant coeurs et pépins. Placez-les au fur et à mesure de l'épluchage dans une jatte contenant de l'eau fraiche.

Quand elles sont toutes préparées, plongez-les 2 minutes dans une grande casserole d'eau bouillante, puis égouttez-les.

Faites fondre le sucre dans les 500 ml d'eau et faites cuire au feu moyen. Au premier bouillon, ajoutez les jus et le zeste du citron, ainsi que la gousse de vanille, fendue en longueur. Mettez-y les poires, et faites cuire à feu vif pendant environ 3/4 heures.

Retirez les zestes avant de mettre en pots. Couvrez.

Durée de conservation: 1 an.

•

CHESTNUT CREAM WITH VANILLA

For twelve 8 ounce jars

4-1/2 pounds chestnuts
1 quart milk
1 vanilla bean
7-1/2 cups granulated sugar
1 cup water

Cut an "X" on top of each chestnut with a knife. Place the chestnuts in a pot and cover with cold water. Bring to a boil and cook for a few minutes. Remove pot from heat and lift out about 10 chestnuts. Quickly remove the outer shell and inner skin of the chestnuts.

Pour milk into a large pot. Split the vanilla bean lengthwise and add to milk. Add the peeled chestnuts and cook over low heat, stirring occasionally, until the chestnuts are cooked and the milk is absorbed. Remove the vanilla bean and set aside. Strain or puree the chestnuts, leaving some pieces, if you wish. Keep this mixture warm.

Combine the sugar and the water in a large pot and cook to soft ball stage. Add the chestnut puree. Scrape the seeds out of the vanilla bean and add them, along with the vanilla bean itself, to the mixture. Stir well and boil for 20 to 30 minutes. The mixture should be quite thick and will stick to a wooden spoon. Remove the vanilla bean and place the chestnut cream in jars.

This Chestnut Cream should keep for one year if properly sealed.

CREME DE MARRONS VANILLEE

Pour 12 pots de 250g

2 kg de marrons, ou bien,
1.5 kg de marrons épluchés
1 l de lait
1 gousse de vanille
1.5 kg de sucre
250 ml d'eau

Faites une incision "X" en travers de chaque marron à l'aide d'un couteau pointu. Mettez les marrons dans une casserole. Couvrez largement d'eau froide. Faites chauffer. Laisser bouillir quelques minutes, retirez la casserole du feu, prenez avec l'écumoire une dizaine de marrons à la fois, et enlevez rapidement l'écorce et la peau qui se détachent facilement ensemble. Si vous prenez des marrons épluchés, vous pouvez éviter cette étape.

Mettez le lait dans une casserole avec la gousse de vanille fendue (en longueur). Ajoutez-y les marrons épluchés et faites les cuire au feu doux, en remuant de temps en temps, jusqu'à l'absorption du lait. Les marrons devraient être bien cuits. Enlevez la gousse de vanille et gardez-la côté. Passez les marrons au mixer ou au tamis, en laissant des morceaux, si vous voulez. Gardez cette purée au chaud.

Faites avec le sucre et l'eau un sirop cuit au "petit boulé." Mettez la purée de marrons dans le sirop. Grattez les grains de vanille de la gousse et ajoutez les au sirop avec la gousse. Remuez bien et faites bouillir pendant 20–30 minutes. La pâte devrait être épaisse et tenir à la cuillère. Retirez la gousse de vanille. Mettez la crème en pots.

Durée de conservation: 1 an.

VANILLA-FLAVORED MANGO CREME

Makes approximately 3 pints

1-3/4 pounds fresh or frozen mango puree, strained
7 ounces heavy cream
1 vanilla bean, split lengthwise
1 cup granulated sugar
8 egg yolks
6 tablespoons cornstarch
2 tablespoons soft butter

In a stainless steel pot, bring the mango puree, cream, vanilla bean, and half the sugar to a boil.

Meanwhile, whisk the egg yolks and the remaining sugar together in a bowl until light (ribbon stage). Sift the cornstarch over the yolks and whisk in.

Pour about one-third of the boiling mango mixture over the egg yolks, whisking constantly. Pour everything back into the pot and cook over medium heat, continuing to whisk constantly. Once the liquid comes to a boil, cook for 10 seconds more, then remove from the heat. Whisk in the butter and allow the cream to cool.

This custard may be used as a replacement for pastry cream.

CREME DE MANGUES VANILLEE

Pour 1.5 kg environ

800 ml de purée de mangues, fraîche ou surgelée (et passé au tamis)
200 ml de créme fluide
1 gousse de vanille, fendue en longueur
200 g de sucre semoule
8 jaunes d'oeuf
80 g de fécule de maïs
30 g de beurre pommade

Dans une casserole en inox, faites bouillir la purée de mangues, la crème, la gousse de vanille et la moitié du sucre.

Dans un bol à l'aide d'un fouet, faites blanchir les jaunes d'oeuf avec le reste du sucre. Tamisez la fécule de maïs là-dessus, et encorporez-la.

Verser un tier du liquide bouillant sur les jaunes, en fouettant bien. Remettez le tout dans la casserole et faites cuire à feu moyen, toujours en fouettant. Laissez bouillir 10 seconds et retirez du feu. Ajoutez-y le beurre, et laissez refroidir.

Vouse pouvez vous servir de cette crème comme de la crème patissière.

●

May We Introduce You To...

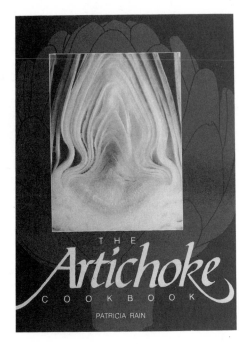

Patricia Rain's *Artichoke Cookbook.*

Patricia Rain spent many years writing and compiling this elegant and beautifully produced book with members of The Artichoke Advisory Boad, growers, distributors, historians, and anyone with a good recipe or story to tell. Living in the heart of the artichoke cultivation area, Patricia Rain couples her unique in-depth perspective with her love of fine food in this book designed for those who have never been served a well-prepared artichoke, and for veteran consumers of this sophisticated thistle.

- numerous illustrations
- history and lore
- cultivation information
- nutrition facts
- how to store artichokes
- how to prepare artichokes
- artichokes and wine
- growing your own
- over 100 recipes for appetizers, soups, salads, cold dishes, hot dishes, sauces, dips, and desserts

How to order *The Artichoke Cookbook:*

This book can be ordered at your local bookstore or directly from the publisher. Send $11.95 (plus $2.50 for shipping); California residents add 8.5% sales tax. Send your check or money order to:

Celestial Arts Publishing
P.O. Box 7327
Berkeley, CA 94707